MY MOTHER, A SERIAL KILLER

MY MOTHER, A SERIAL KILLER

HAZEL BARON & JANET FIFE-YEOMANS

HarperCollins*Publishers*

HarperCollins*Publishers*
First published in Australia in 2018
This edition published in 2020
by HarperCollins*Publishers* Australia Pty Limited
ABN 36 009 913 517
harpercollins.com.au

HarperCollins*Publishers*
Level 13, 201 Elizabeth Street, Sydney NSW 2000, Australia
Unit D1, 63 Apollo Drive, Rosedale, Auckland 0632, New Zealand
A 53, Sector 57, Noida, UP, India
1 London Bridge Street, London SE1 9GF, United Kingdom
Bay Adelaide Centre, East Tower, 22 Adelaide Street West, 41st floor, Toronto,
    Ontario M5H 4E3, Canada
195 Broadway, New York NY 10007, USA

A catalogue record for this book is available
from the National Library of Australia

ISBN 978 1 4607 5843 4 (paperback)
ISBN 978 1 4607 0891 0 (ebook)

Cover design by Brianna Benton
Cover photography by Lisa Fotios
Typeset in Sabon LT Std by Kirby Jones

I would like to dedicate this book to my husband, Bill, who my whole life has shown me love and support; to my children, who lost out on a lot of regular family life because of the many trips to court over a period of five years; to my many friends who stood by me through thick and thin and made sure that I always felt their love and support, which kept me going; and to my co author, Janet Fife-Yeomans, who has made all this real. I think she has really nailed it.

— Hazel Baron

CONTENTS

PROLOGUE

'WOMAN ON THREE MURDER CHARGES!' THE PAPERBOY SHOUTED as the cars pulled up at the traffic lights on Sydney's busy Crown Street.

Hazel Baron didn't need to see the headlines on Monday afternoon's *Daily Mirror* to know who they were written about. She didn't need to see the photograph of the alleged killer on the front page to know who she was. It was her mother.

In true tabloid fashion, the front page was almost entirely taken up by the photograph. A woman on one murder charge would always guarantee such a spread, never mind a woman accused of being a triple killer. Dressed in a conservative overcoat, gloves and hat, despite the heat of the December day, Hazel Dulcie Bodsworth, fifty-two, had been snapped as she was led by detectives from Sydney Airport. She looked every inch the respectable middle-aged woman, not a hair out of place, not a stray emotion. But Dulcie, as she was known, and her scandalously young husband Henry William Bodsworth, nineteen years her junior, had been extradited from Melbourne to face Sydney's Central Local Court. Dulcie was charged with murdering three men, Henry with murdering one of them 'with his wife'.

Hazel Baron was terrified, exhilarated and nauseated, all at once.

'Read all about it!' the paperboy shouted through the passenger window, trying to sell another copy.

'No thanks,' Hazel said, shaking her head in a quick way that was little more than a shiver.

Her husband, Bill, looked over at her from the driver's seat and asked her: 'Are you all right? Did you see Dulcie?'

Hazel cradled her arms tighter around the two-week-old baby boy she and Bill had just collected from Crown Street Women's Hospital. In 1964, there were no laws banning babies from the front seat of a car. A few weeks earlier, the couple had applied to adopt another much-wanted child as a sibling for their daughter. They had been told the wait would be about two years and expected it to be even longer as their rural town, Wilcannia, was way back in the northwest of New South Wales almost 1000 kilometres from Sydney. But here they were leaving the state's largest maternity hospital to drive home with their six-pound bundle of joy on the very day the whole city was talking about Dulcie Bodsworth, the triple murderer. Talk about joy and despair colliding. The young mother looked down at her new baby and a strange feeling of peace came over her. In the busy traffic, she had an 'out of body' feeling. It was as though she had been tapped on the shoulder by a spirit or an angel.

No one who knew Hazel would think of her as religious; she even described herself as a bit of a rough diamond at times. Religion, she always thought, was personal and better kept under wraps, but at that moment, she felt that if she put her faith in God, she knew she would cope. She felt that God was looking after her and had given her the baby at the right time.

'Hazel.' Bill's voice dragged her back to reality on that day, 8 December 1964. 'Did you see Dulcie?'

Hazel turned and, very calmly, said: 'Yes.'

The truth wasn't always nice but it was always the truth. The truth was that it was Hazel who had dobbed her mother in. The truth was that she knew her mother would have kept on killing if she had not been caught.

But the courage it had taken Hazel to step forward was ebbing away as the reality hit, splashed across the front page of a newspaper. Bill was her tower of strength, the rock she could always lean on, but it was Hazel who would have to stand up in court and give evidence against her mother and her stepfather if they pleaded not guilty. Even worse was how terrified she felt at how Dulcie would react when she found out Hazel was behind it. Or if Dulcie was acquitted and freed.

In the heat of that summer day, Hazel was happy about her new baby and scared about her mother's fate, sweating and shivering, all at the same time.

CHAPTER ONE

TED BARON

HAZEL BARON WAS NINE WHEN SHE FIRST SUSPECTED HER mother was a murderer.

The tall gangly schoolgirl with short curly hair who wore long socks, wool skirts which came to below her knees and heavy knitted sweaters was already the keeper of too many of her mother's secrets.

Don't tell your dad about this. Don't tell your dad about that. Don't tell him about the sneaky hours in the dark on the big back seat of the family's American-built Nash car with young Harry, nineteen years her mother's junior. Harry was only supposed to be 'helping with the kids'. As a kid herself, Hazel did what she was told and never even considered telling on her mum. Dulcie was also quick with her right hand to dish out a slap or worse. In those days, no one questioned using corporal punishment to keep children in line.

Looking back, Hazel's suspicions should have been aroused on the night when her mother, Dulcie, then known as Hazel Dulcie Baron, gave the kids warm milk and Aspro tablets before bed. It was the first time in their lives that Hazel, her brother Allan, eight, and the five-year-old twins, Margaret and Jim, had been given warm milk to drink. Dulcie wasn't much of a mollycoddling mother, treating her four children more like mini grown-ups. But this had been a big day, she said, and the milk and Aspros would help them sleep. Her attention made them all feel special for a change.

It was the dying days of the winter of 1950 and the Baron family's home was two old army tents made out of heavy green canvas set up on the northern bank of the Murray River. The breeze coming off the water made the night air even chillier but Dulcie never seemed to feel the cold. As the kids sat with their blankets around themselves, keeping warm by the campfire, Dulcie just pulled the cardigan she wore over her dress closer to her chest. It was quiet and dark as she heated the milk in a pan over the burning logs, the only light the sparks flying up. The ribbons of smoke twisted into the air like ghost gums along the riverbanks. Hazel could just make out the outlines of their two tents a few metres away at the edge of their camp.

Hazel didn't know where the tents had come from; they just turned up. Dulcie was a wonderful storyteller and she rarely let the facts get in the way. Hazel figured her mum had probably charmed someone with one of her hard-luck stories, of which she had many; she had them all down pat and they were invariably successful. In the 1940s she had done her bit for the war effort, cooking for the soldiers who were training for the army at Bonegilla army camp in northeast Victoria near Wodonga while the family lived nearby. In 1947, Bonegilla had become Australia's first migrant reception centre and Hazel thought her mum had probably hustled the tents from there as army surplus. Even now, at forty-one, Dulcie could really turn it on. That persuasive little-girl-lost routine, all helpless and in need of a man to save her — it never failed.

As it turned out, it was the men who needed to be saved from her.

The family had pitched their tents about a month earlier on the flat lands of Buronga, on the New South Wales side of the river, which faced the Victorian town of Mildura. Their closest neighbours were other nomadic families living in similar post-World War II straitened circumstances in tents further along the riverbank. Dulcie was pleasant to them; she cared what other people thought about her and she liked to be liked. She always had a smile and a hello when they passed each other, but that was as far as it went. She preferred to keep herself to herself and told the kids to do the same. Mind what you say. Careful what you tell people. Wherever they went, Dulcie built fences around them with smiles and reassurances.

Hazel already suspected that their family might not be quite normal but she really had nothing to compare it with. Everyone had their secrets, didn't they?

There wasn't much to do at night in the bush when home was a tent without a light so this night, as on all the others, it was early to bed. There were no luxuries in their lives but they never wanted for the basics. Wooden crates were used to stack clothes and beds were mattresses on the tarpaulin floor. The two girls, Hazel and Margaret, shared a double mattress in one corner of the tent while the boys slept head to toe on a single mattress in another corner. Ever resourceful, Dulcie would reuse the hessian bags which in those days were used for flour and sugar; she stitched them together into what were called waggas, but because they were too scratchy to use as blankets on their own, they had to be covered in material from the op shop. If she couldn't get pieces of cloth large enough to cover them in one go, Dulcie got the cheapest dresses, unstitched them so she didn't lose any of the cloth and hand-stitched patchwork covers for the bags. They were the cheapest doonas and common among shearers and families like the Barons doing it tough.

Dulcie could conjure up anything from nothing, just like the tents. And the truth.

The reason for the warm milk and Aspros was snoring on a stretcher bed near the tent flap. Wednesday, 30 August 1950, had been a big day because their dad, Ted Baron, forty-eight, had come home from hospital.

The once-powerful railway ganger, who had led teams of tough men doing hard graft across New South Wales and Victoria, was just a shadow of himself. He had arrived at camp that afternoon in a taxi from Mildura Base Hospital, over the Murray River Bridge and down to Buronga. Dulcie had been dutifully visiting him every day for the two weeks her husband was in Mildura Hospital and when he told her that he wanted to go home with her, she seemed suitably thrilled.

Ted couldn't really afford a taxi fare but, crippled with rheumatoid arthritis, he could hardly get around, even with a walking stick. He had had a tough time of it for a few years, in and out of hospitals in various towns as doctors tried all sorts of treatments, including the new-fangled 'gold injections' which were supposed to help the pain and swelling in his hands, feet and legs but to which Ted had an adverse reaction. There was no cure for his condition and he knew it was only going to get worse, something he accepted in a matter-of-fact way as people did in those days, at least the people he knew. You didn't expect too much from life and took what was given you. Ted was a no-nonsense conservative fellow, not the kind of man to make a fuss.

Ted was still tall at six feet two inches and wore his only suit, a dark brown one, with the pants held up with braces. He would never wear a belt, believing the only 'proper' pants were ones with braces. But despite the braces, the jacket and pants that had once fitted his big frame were now hanging loose. His illness, coupled with typical hospital food, had stripped about a stone from what had been a fifteen-stone frame. But Ted was still a handsome man, his high forehead and hair that was still dark and curly making him look younger than his years even as the pain in his gnarled hands and feet never receded.

He didn't like that he had been a bit of a poor excuse for a dad in recent years. The twins had barely known him when he had been able to chase them, give them piggybacks and pick them up and tickle them till they cried as he had with Hazel and Allan. The two oldest remembered the jokes he would tell, never in bad taste, never using a swear word, but oh so funny.

He had provided well for them until he couldn't work any longer. Hazel never knew how her mum and dad met but when he and Dulcie married in 1940, they had a house on Route Road, Wodonga, before they moved to John Street, Beechworth, the only real home Hazel remembered. Her dad had painted the outside of the house green and the green front door opened onto a white hallway with four bedrooms off it. Their only warmth came from a kerosene heater in the kitchen and there was always a bottle of kerosene on the bench. By the time the 1949 census came around, Ted, to his own shame, had to list himself as 'unemployed'. Dulcie told the census-taker she was on 'home duties', as did a lot of women of the day. As the rent money dried up that year, the family moved into a caravan at Wangaratta. The tents were the final step as they slipped into poverty. Now he couldn't even put food on the table for them. But they were still his world, all he had, and he loved them dearly. He had a broad smile on his face as he ambled towards his four children that day when he came home from the hospital.

The kids had got used to their dad being in hospital and they surrounded him and walked him back to the camp. While they were happy to see him, their welcome couldn't rival that of Ted's dog, Toby, an Australian terrier, who threw himself at his master, whirling in circles at Ted's feet and whimpering with excitement.

Dulcie was kindness incarnate to her husband that afternoon, fussing over him and making sure he was comfortable, much to young Hazel's surprise. She gave Hazel and Allan some change and sent them to the corner shop at the end of the gravel road along the riverbank to get the milk and Aspros. Money was always tight and milk was a real treat in itself; they usually drank their tea black. For two shillings (around 20c today), they could buy a loaf of bread and enough hot chips to make chip sandwiches for them all. A family feast. Most nights, dinner was stew made from cheap cuts of meat that were only edible once they had been cooked slowly over the fire or in the camp oven.

Hazel and her brothers and sister never saw their growing up as being poor; they didn't know they had been living in poverty for over twelve months. They just took it in their stride, as kids do. On the other side of the river, the lights of Mildura twinkled in the distance. Even in 1950 Mildura was classed as a city. While to the locals it still seemed like a big country town, to the four Baron children it seemed as big a city as Sydney or Melbourne and they hadn't even dreamt of going there. No one they knew had ever been as far as the capital cities.

Their campsite was about as basic as it got with a folding camp table to eat meals off and oil drums or logs as chairs. The public toilets were a fair walk away and when they needed water for the kettle or to wash and the water tank was empty, the kids just walked the five metres from the tents to the river with a bowl to scoop up the water and bring it back. Their mum always told them to watch what they were doing because the Murray was not only murky and wide, it was deep, especially in August of 1950, swollen with the rains from what had been the wettest winter for years. The river was running about three-quarters full but it was still almost four metres deep in the middle, she warned, at least that deep.

He might have been crippled with arthritis but Ted Baron wasn't stupid. Harry, real name Henry Bodsworth, was still hanging around their camp. Harry, twenty-two, had joined their little family at the start of the year during Ted's bouts in hospitals, first in Wangaratta and then in Albury. He had helped them move to the Murray, piling their belongings on a trailer that Dulcie towed behind their big, black car, the old Nash with running boards, even as Ted was back in hospital in Albury.

Harry looked more like sixteen than twenty-two and was prone to the giggles, which kept Dulcie entertained no end. He made Hazel feel like the grown-up of the family. To give him his due, he was young and healthy enough to work hard. He also had no idea how old Dulcie really was because she had been lying about her age for years. When she married Ted Baron in 1940, she listed her age on their marriage certificate as twenty-six — when she was really thirty-one — and those five years she shaved off her age followed her through life.

'He's got no family and no home,' Dulcie told Ted. And anyway, because of his illness, Ted wasn't around to be the breadwinner and while Dulcie did some cleaning for cash in hand, they needed the money Harry brought in when he got a job here and there. Ted didn't like the situation that Dulcie had created. He tried to stand up to her and he knew he should have done more about it but pain had robbed him of most of his resolve. He rarely raised his voice to Dulcie and was never much of a match for her when she began. In the end, Dulcie always got her own way.

Ted slouched on the bed soon after arriving back at camp while Dulcie fussed and fluffed about. He may well have wondered what he had done to deserve it but all he could think of was that if he went to sleep, the pain would go away. It was the only comfort he got these days. Dulcie suggested he turn in for the night before the kids did. She told him to stay in what was usually her bed, a camp bed on legs in the kids' tent, and she would take one of the thin shearer's mattresses on the floor. Ted got no rest without sleeping tablets, even though they made him snore. As he lay in bed, Dulcie brought him one of their best china teacups full of water so he could wash them down. She pulled the wagga up around his neck and tucked him in at 6 pm.

He was sound asleep when the kids got into their beds. Hazel bent down and gave his lined cheek a kiss but he didn't move. As for the kids, the warm milk and Aspros had the desired effect and they slept like logs.

Hazel's mum shook her awake the next morning. The flap to the tent was ajar, the shaft of light showing that her dad's bed was empty. Dulcie was bending over her, her face all teary: 'Hazel, Hazel. Your father's gone. He wasn't here when I woke up. I think he fell in the river and drowned last night.'

In her hand, she held the china teacup.

'I think he went down to the water to get a drink and fell in. I don't know what else could have happened. We've got to look for him. Come on, get up and help.'

On the banks of the river, Ted's faithful dog, Toby, howled into the morning air.

Once the kids were up, Dulcie ran to the corner shop to use their phone and call the police. It was barely 8 am when the first officers arrived. They found the four children peeping through the flap of the big tent, their faces fearful at what had happened, their mother in tears, their father missing and his dog, sitting unmoving on the sandy riverbank, staring out at the water and still howling. A young man introduced as Harry was wafting a flame until it caught on under a pile of hefty logs in the fireplace.

Dulcie wrapped her arms across her chest as she spoke to the officers, tucking her hands under her arms. You couldn't call her pretty but she was an attractive woman, who wore her confidence in her face. She was always ladylike and demure; and, despite having little money to spend on clothes, she did her best to look classy. You would never get a flash of her petticoat because her dresses were always below the knee. Dulcie was five feet six inches with ginger hair that she kept short, as was the fashion. She wore thick glasses but she couldn't read very well. However, she could talk — boy, could she talk.

Her words came pouring out. Her husband had got home from hospital just yesterday afternoon, Dulcie told the police. He was a cripple who used to use a wheelchair but she had returned it to the hospital. He'd been fine when he went to bed in his pyjamas and she had heard him moving around about 1.30 am. She had slipped back to sleep and, when she woke at 6 am, she saw he wasn't in the tent. He'd gone.

She went looking for him, knowing he couldn't have gone far in his state. In the sand on the banks of the river she had found the cup. Oh my God, she was afraid that in his enfeebled state he had got up for a drink and fallen in. Or he might have committed suicide, she said, as bad as that sounded. The gold injections he had been given for his arthritis could send you mental if they didn't cure you, Dulcie had heard, and she was happy to pass that on to the police.

In his police notebook, one of the officers took down the details: Edwin James Gray Baron, born 11 January 1902, at

Black Dog Creek, Chiltern, Victoria. Six feet two inches, about fourteen stone. Last seen the previous evening wearing a singlet and pyjamas.

As Harry got the fire going to chase the morning chill from the air, Dulcie introduced him to the constables as Harry Boyd. Harry said he was Ted's younger brother. Listening from the tent, Hazel had no idea where that name came from. She stayed silent. Harry nodded to the officers and shook their hands. He and Ted were close and he was frantic about what had happened to him, he wanted them to know.

The police took charge. They called in reinforcements and every day for the next two weeks, they searched the bushes and the shoreline along the banks downriver. The other campers further up the riverbank were shocked to hear about Dulcie's ill husband going missing and joined police and other locals in the search. Apart from the china cup, the only sign of Ted Baron was his false teeth. A few days after he disappeared, Dulcie showed them to Hazel, green weed wrapped around the teeth like roots. She said she had found them by the edge of the water not far from the camp.

The police officers felt genuinely sorry for the mother of four who was obviously struggling to keep any roof over her family's head, even a canvas roof. They told Mrs Baron they would do all they could to find her husband but as the days passed, they had to be honest: hope was running out.

Among the searchers were Captain Bill Collins and his brother Norm, two of the five 'river rat' children born into the famous Murray River family of 'Pop' and Amy Collins.

It had been five decades since the Murray, Australia's longest river, had been a busy water highway, its paddle steamers linking the pioneering pastoralists in the heart of New South Wales with the rest of the world. One of the river's most loved paddle boats was the *Avoca*. Built in 1877, it had carried cargo, flour from the mills, and helped transport the machinery to build the locks on the Murray. It was such a stalwart of the era that after it sank in 1921, it was never forgotten. The Collins brothers bought the raised vessel and reinvigorated it as a showboat for tourists.

One or other of them was at the helm of the *Avoca* every day of the year, spring, summer, autumn, winter. The families camping along the banks of the river became familiar figures to the brothers who didn't always know their names but recognised their faces and their individual campsites. They saw the new faces who took their places as families moved on, chasing work in an endless circle.

On Tuesday, 12 September, Bill, forty-two, a master mariner and shipwright, was repairing the boat on the riverbank when he heard shouting. He looked up to see three men on the opposite bank waving their arms.

'Hey, over there! Bloody hell, mate, have you got a boat? There's a body floating in the water!'

The men pointed downstream where Captain Bill could see a body drifting slowly in the current south of the Mildura bridge, about 500 or 600 yards away. He took the *Avoca* out and, as gently as he could, pushed the body back to the bank. After twelve days in the water, it was grotesque, bloated, missing a leg and with a shoe on its remaining foot. The captain could still see it was a man. He shouted to his brother to help.

They figured Ted Baron had just been found and called the police.

About thirty kilometres further up the Murray River, at Wentworth police station, Constable William John Corby took the call at 3.15 pm that day. At twenty-nine, Corby was an RAAF veteran of World War II who had followed in the footsteps of his dad Stanley and joined the police when the war ended. He had been posted to Collector and then to his current job just a few months earlier, moving into the police house with his wife and their then four-year-old son. Life as a country cop suited him well. He was a solid, reliable officer. Corby was called in because the government medical officer, Dr James Ross Morris, himself a war veteran, was based at Wentworth and the body would have to be taken there for a postmortem examination. Constable Corby drove into Mildura where it had been arranged that he would meet Harry 'Boyd' at the morgue in Mildura Base Hospital.

Harry was waiting for him. He told the constable that Dulcie was his sister and that he had known Ted as his brother-in-law for about twelve years. As anyone who lies for a living knows, you have to have a good memory to be a good liar. Harry was an amateur. Dulcie, on the other hand, was a liar by nature and could easily slip from one role to the next mainly because she believed what she was saying at the time. Luckily for both of them, none of the police called Harry out on his slip-up.

'Ted's been suffering from rheumatoid arthritis for some time, the poor bugger, but my sister, Mrs Baron, can tell you more about that. She's also got an idea of how he came to be in the river,' Harry told Constable Corby.

At 5 pm that day beneath the bright cold lights of the morgue, Ted Baron's body on a slab was officially identified by the man who had been having an affair with his wife, now his widow. If Harry felt any guilt, he didn't show it; and Corby was not expecting any guilt so he never looked for it.

That evening, Corby accompanied the body back to Wentworth. The young constable had seen a few autopsies by that time so it didn't unduly bother him to be present as a witness when

Dr Morris cut open Ted Baron at Wentworth District Hospital that night. His air passages were full of fluid, showing he had been alive when he went into the river. The medical officer recorded the cause of death as asphyxia from drowning and estimated the body had been in the water for between seven and twelve days.

By laws that have barely changed for hundreds of years, all sudden or violent deaths or deaths from unknown causes have to be reported to the coroner. The Wentworth District Coroner at the time was Murray Farquhar and while he would be determining Ted Baron's cause of death, the investigation was in the hands of Constable Corby. The officer never had any doubt that Ted had drowned but as protocol demanded, he had to prepare a brief of evidence. So the next day, he was back in Mildura to interview the widow, Hazel Dulcie Baron.

Dulcie had kept the kids home from the local Catholic school since their dad had gone missing. She told them it was for their own good as she didn't want them to be upset by all the questions the other children would have — questions which she didn't want them to have to answer. She needed to be in control and keeping the children at home ensured that. The twins Margaret and Jim were still too young to understand what was going on. Their family was always on the move, they lived out of boxes, they couldn't make friends and their only permanents had been their mum and dad. Now their dad had gone and as much as being sad, all four of them were scared and puzzled.

Their mum told them they would only be tormented if they went to school so best to stay away. Nobody from the school came to check on the four Baron children; they had barely been going to the local classrooms for a month by then and the welfare authorities were not nearly as sophisticated as they are today. To fill in their days, there was nothing much else for the children to do except walk around, catch bugs, throw sticks in the river and see whose floated away the fastest, or throw in a piece of string and pretend they were fishing. Anything to stay out of the way of the police, of the authorities, of the neighbours. Anything to stay out of the way of anyone and everyone.

The reason the kids had been peeking through the tent flap when the police arrived that first day was because Dulcie had ordered them to stay inside. She told Constable Corby they were too upset and, as a father himself, he understood. On top of that, there was no reason for the police to suspect otherwise.

The only questions the constable had for Dulcie were perfunctory but he had to ask them in order to record an official statement. She replied as he went through them. She and Ted had married after they had known each other for a few months. Their oldest, Hazel, had come along in 1941 and then the other kids followed. She had no idea how they would cope but they would get on with things. Oh yes, Dulcie could talk. She liked to appear helpless but she was always totally in charge.

She told the officer they were planning to bury Ted the next day.

As the family had no money, they had been granted a pauper's funeral at the Presbyterian Church in Mildura. Dulcie told Hazel to stay home and look after her brothers and sister. Funerals were no place for kids, she said. It was also another ploy to keep them away from people.

The Barons hadn't been brought up a particularly religious family. Ted had been a Presbyterian who had started going to Catholic churches after one particular stay in hospital where the local priest who regularly came around the wards had been a jolly fat man — a lot more fun than the po-faced Protestants, he had thought. Despite that, Ted was given a burial spot in the Protestant graveyard.

Ted had been an only child from solid settler stock. Ted's father, James Baron, had been born on a ship as his young parents, aged in their twenties, sailed from Cheshire for Australia for a new life. Although he had died a few years earlier from a heart attack while chopping wood, Hazel could just about remember visiting him and her grandmother Agnes, known as Aggie, on their farm at Black Dog Creek, Chiltern, in Victoria's northeast. Agnes Baron was a lovely lady who wore her grey hair in a bun and always had an apron on because she seemed to be constantly cooking. It was from her that Hazel got her middle name, Hazel Agnes Baron, and she was sometimes called Aggie herself.

Aggie was still alive, as were Ted's father's two brothers, his uncles Ralph and John, and there was a big family of cousins and aunts and uncles around Beechworth and Chiltern. Dulcie told none of them about Ted's death. The only mourners on 14 September 1950 were Harry and an apparently tear-stained Dulcie. After a short service, they left. Ted's grave was abandoned, unadorned.

Ted Baron was dead and buried but the clerical work that accompanies sudden death still had to be completed.

A week later, the four children were still not back at school and they watched as Dulcie and Harry got into Dulcie's car, the big Nash. As Hazel heard the car doors slam and the engine start up, it made her feel lonely. The inquest into their dad's death was being heard on Friday, 22 September, at Wentworth Courthouse and Hazel, once again, was left in charge of the kids. Dulcie told her they were too young to accompany them to court.

Dulcie and Harry sat on the hard, wooden benches outside the beautiful 1880 Wentworth Court building waiting to give evidence, careful not to hold hands or show affection of that kind. Constable Corby had explained to them what was to happen at the inquest.

Inquests are held to officially determine the identity of the deceased, when and where that person died and the manner as well as the cause of death. With about a murder a year at Wentworth, the coroner, Murray Farquhar, was no stranger to homicide but there was no indication that Ted Baron's inquest was going to be anything but run of the mill. There was no history of violence in his life and no evidence of violence in his death. Nevertheless, the coroner was thorough and spent two days having witnesses questioned.

First up was Dr Morris. His medical reports and statement were tendered to the court and his time in the witness box was short. He testified that he had been the government medical officer at Wentworth for eighteen years and the body he had been told was that of Ted Baron had drowned. Ted's medical records from Mildura Base Hospital were also tendered to the court confirming he had suffered badly from rheumatoid arthritis, but they couldn't shed any light on his cause of death. Despite the mental anguish his medical condition entailed, there was no evidence he had been suicidal.

Dr Morris was followed by Constable Corby who, as the officer in charge of the investigation, gave the court an overview of what had happened and testified that Harry Boyd had identified the body as that of his brother-in-law Ted Baron. Having given his evidence, Corby could then sit in court and assist the coroner.

The three men who had spotted the body in the river were called to testify to what they had seen, followed by Captain Bill Collins, who was as succinct in court as he had been in his statement to the police. A man of few words, he said he had spotted the body he now knew to be Ted Baron's after being alerted to it by three men who were strangers to him. The body had still been wearing pyjamas.

When Dulcie was called into the witness box, she reiterated the story she had given to the police and which she had sworn to in her statement. She and Ted Baron had married on 1 June 1940, at Wangaratta in Victoria. She had last seen him when she went to bed on the last night he was alive and found him missing from his bed when she got up at six the next morning.

The inquest was adjourned over the weekend and Harry was the last witness on the Monday. He told the court how he was Dulcie's brother and that he recalled Ted being in good spirits when he returned from hospital on 30 August. Harry said Ted and Dulcie had discussed general family matters, about how the kids were, that kind of stuff, until he went to bed.

Coroner Farquhar wound up the inquest, giving his commiserations to Dulcie and recording a verdict of accidental death.

Still no one picked up on the fact that Harry had somehow morphed from Ted's brother to his brother-in-law or questioned where the surname Boyd had come from. Perhaps the police officer who was initially told that had not recorded it in his notebook because he never recalled it later.

Every girl needs her mum. A young girl's relationship with her mother shapes her life; it makes her what she is whether for good or bad. It's a complex but powerful bond that no one outside it can ever understand, psychiatrists and psychologists included — even though they may profess that they can provide insights. It is personal and all-encompassing.

While Dulcie was crying and appeared to be really grieving while the police were around, Hazel wasn't her mother's daughter for nothing. She lacked her mother's cunning but she picked up the indications that all was not as it seemed. She was suspicious even if she wasn't sure exactly what had happened to her dad.

Hazel noticed that when the family was alone again, her mum was nervous and on edge. She had heard her mum tell the police Harry was her brother and then Harry said he was Ted's brother but Hazel knew Harry wasn't their uncle from either side of the family. She knew enough about life to know that her mother shouldn't have been sharing the small tent every night with Harry, except of course when her dad was home and she slept with the kids.

Now, Hazel noticed Dulcie and Harry arguing a lot, for the first time in their relationship. A few days after the inquest, Hazel was sitting on the end of her mattress in the tent stitching up a hole in one of the boys' woollen socks. The other kids were away playing marbles or hopscotch and Dulcie didn't realise Hazel wasn't with them.

From inside the tent, she overheard Dulcie and Harry talking about 'getting our story right'. For several days, Toby the terrier had continued to bark and howl at the river and would not be silenced.

'If that bloody dog could talk, we would be dead,' Dulcie said.

Hazel couldn't move or she would give herself away. She didn't even realise that she was holding her breath. She knew she had heard something she wasn't supposed to have heard.

Not long after, Dulcie and Harry told the kids that Toby had run away. Hazel didn't believe them.

While Hazel looked like their mum, Allan took after his dad, tall and stocky but with sandy hair. He was the shy one of the kids, much quieter and less self-assured than Hazel, who they all looked up to. Hazel became more fearful when Allan confided in his big sister that the day their dad had arrived home from hospital, he had heard his dad say to their mum: 'I saw him kiss you.'

Although his dad did not mention a name, Allan knew he had been talking about Harry.

Allan had said that he had heard Dulcie try to brush it off, laughing: 'Don't be silly, Ed, he did not.'

The police had never spoken to the kids but even if they had, it was doubtful the siblings would have thought to mention what they had heard. Yet, once heard, they could never unhear those words.

The four kids went back to school but Buronga wasn't going to be their home for much longer. Hazel heard her mum tell Harry that because the drowning had been in all the Victorian newspapers, she thought they had better move on because Ted's relatives would be looking for them.

Hazel had stopped loving her mum after her dad's body was retrieved, once his death was confirmed and he was never coming home from any hospital again. She didn't actually tell her mum that in so many words but she became much quieter than she had been. On the other hand, Dulcie seemed to need her oldest daughter even more. Harry replaced 'your dad' as the person Hazel was to keep secrets from. Before they left Buronga, Dulcie casually dropped one more secret into a conversation with Hazel. It seemed that she needed someone to talk to and young Hazel was that person.

She had been married before Ted, she said, but she had never told him. Dulcie and her first husband had had four children but she had no idea where her husband or the children were. Hazel thought her mum looked sad. Dulcie said that someone had to know the truth in case anything happened to her but she did not tell Hazel what to do with the information. Looking back, Hazel thought this was another instance of Dulcie's selfishness — she needed to unburden herself so she dumped the secret on her daughter.

The bombshell was followed by the customary warning, slightly altered: 'Don't tell Harry.'

Hazel knew she would never call Dulcie her mother again.

CHAPTER TWO

DULCIE AND HARRY

HAZEL WASN'T THE FIRST OF DULCIE'S DAUGHTERS TO BE GIVEN that name. Dulcie had called one of the two daughters from her first marriage Hazel as well. When Hazel Baron found that out, it was like getting second prize, or being second-hand. Knowing that she wasn't the 'first choice' hurt even more than having two half-sisters and two half-brothers she had never met. She knew Dulcie liked to stretch the truth — but her story about having had a secret family before meeting Ted Baron was true.

Dulcie was born in the amusingly named Victorian town of Korumburra — amusing because it is said to be an Aboriginal word for maggot. As well as the big fat earthworms that gave the town its name, Korumburra was home in 1909 to miner Charles Ray Ramage, known as Jack, and his wife Dulcie. Their daughter Hazel Dulcie Ramage was born on 12 June that year, an only child.

It would be more than twenty years until Korumburra got a hospital and like almost all the babies until then, Dulcie was born at home, one of the hundreds of babies delivered by the town's much-loved midwife, Irish-born Nora Walmsley. For over fifty years, the nurse — better known by townsfolk as 'Grannie' — had been there day and night for the mothers giving birth. It was said that she turned no one down. Like Dulcie, her mother had little time for officialdom and Dulcie's birth was never registered, which was not unusual for the time. Dulcie kept her real age quiet all her life and it was not until she died that Hazel discovered it through the information Dulcie had given to Centrelink.

Korumburra was a real pioneering East Gippsland town, built on coal and timber mills and, by the time Dulcie was born, the dairy industry. Now it's just a 90-minute drive from Melbourne, 105 kilometres northwest, but in 1909, a train trip on the railroad that passed through town was much more comfortable than going by horse and cart — if you could afford the fare.

There were a couple of banks, churches, a post office and businesses like coach-builders and bakeries that kept the population of around 2000 well catered for. Mrs Henderson's 22-room 'coffee palace' provided much-needed accommodation. Visitors from Melbourne noted the absence of snobbery and it was true that there were few local families who were affluent in those days before dairy and agriculture brought the area its wealth.

At the community's heart were waves of European migrants but Dulcie's mother was second-generation Australian. Hazel never knew whereabouts on the other side of the world the family was originally from because Dulcie rarely talked about her own mother. She had taken off while Dulcie was still young, abandoning her daughter. The Ramage family described her as 'flighty', a polite way to explain why a young woman — who was probably bored and craving adventures beyond a dusty Victorian town — had just up and left.

Hazel met her maternal grandmother only once but she left an indelible impression for all the wrong reasons. It was after her father died and Hazel was eleven or twelve when Dulcie took her to visit her grandmother, who was living on the outskirts of Melbourne. She may have been good-looking forty years earlier but by that time she had well and truly let herself go. She was a fat, squat, formless woman with black hair tied in a scruffy ponytail and a cigarette hanging out of her mouth, living in an old dark house that stank of cigarette smoke and urine. Hazel couldn't wait to get away from her.

As a result of her mother's leaving, young Dulcie was passed around among relatives, of which there were plenty in town including Uncle John, who was the local baker, and his wife, Aunt Agnes. She grew up in many households, none of which she really called 'home'. Hazel always thought that it was her mother's lack of a solid upbringing which sowed the seeds of her restless nature, the reason why she grew up a bit of a gypsy, never being able to settle too long in one place or even with one person. She was also as careless with her own children as her own mother had been with her. Then again, perhaps like the mother who abandoned her, she was also always searching for something better.

Another factor that may have contributed to Dulcie's character was a history of mental illness in the family — one of her grandmothers had died in the notorious Ararat Lunatic Asylum. While Dulcie was never diagnosed with a mental illness herself, Hazel wondered if there was something genetic that caused her mother's selfishness, her lack of empathy that allowed her to live her life doing what she wanted without showing signs of guilt or even feeling any remorse.

Dulcie didn't have much formal education although she did attend the school in Korumburra, which had over 300 pupils. Like most girls in those days in her social class, her basic talents were knowing how to sew and cook and keep house. Most children left school at fifteen in those days and at that age Dulcie headed off to travel, finding work doing what she did best, cooking and cleaning.

On her travels, she met the man who would become her first husband, Edward Cavanagh, known as Ted (like her second husband). He came from the Victorian town of Terang, southwest of Melbourne and about 330 kilometres away from Korumburra. Dulcie always had an escape route, a plan B, throughout her life. Ted Cavanagh was her first — she married him to escape the confines of her home town.

A child of 1911, he was two years younger than Dulcie but, unlike with the men later in her life, she could never boss him around. Ted was a man who liked to take charge. Like her, he was a bit wild. He loved women and never really liked hard work.

*

When Dulcie was marrying Cavanagh, Henry William Bodsworth was just a baby. He was born on 20 July 1928 in Hopetoun, 400 kilometres northwest of Melbourne in the heart of the Southern Mallee. Known as Harry from the day he was born, he was the third eldest in a traditionally big family of nine children with six brothers and two sisters. His father worked as a milkman but, like Dulcie, Harry was brought up in a broken home. His parents split up in 1939, when he was eleven and his mother Louisa was thirty-two. He went to live with his mum.

Harry left school at thirteen and worked as a farm labourer on various properties around Victoria, going where there was work even at such a young age. On 22 March 1946, at the age of seventeen, he did what many young men did and lied to join the military, putting his age up by a year when he enlisted for

World War II at Watsonia, in Melbourne's northeast, the closest office to where he was working at the time. His war record for service number VX501363 shows his year of birth as 1927 and his nationality as British, his parents' home country. His mother had married again and was then Louisa Pill, living with Harry's stepfather in Victoria Street, Altona, on the outskirts of Melbourne.

Harry spent over two years as a member of the Australian Infantry Force working as a signalman, six of those months with the occupation forces in Japan, but he never really saw action. His only injury while in the army wasn't at the hands of the enemy. It happened while he was based with American and British forces at 1 Base Signal Park, Warwick Farm, which is now Warwick Racecourse. At dusk on 12 February 1947, Harry was walking along the Great Western Highway towards Penrith on Sydney's western outskirts when he was knocked down by a civilian vehicle and woke up in Nepean District Hospital. The accident left him with a small wound on the right side of his scalp but he was back fit for duty just five days later.

He was honourably discharged in April 1948, a month after arriving back from the port of Kure, at the entrance to Hiroshima Bay, on the HMAS *Kanimbla*.

Like too many servicemen and women, his skills counted for next to nothing when he returned to civilian life but Harry at least found one of the few jobs that were always available at the time. He became a rabbit trapper. Rabbit meat and skins were big business and the trappers also helped homeowners and farmers trying to keep in check the pest that had become a plague since being introduced into Australia with the First Fleet in 1788. As he had before his stint in the forces, Harry went where work took him throughout Victoria until he got a job as a transport driver in early 1949.

In April that year, he was almost killed. Harry was changing a tyre on his semi-trailer when the rim blew off the wheel and smashed into his forehead. He was rushed to Wangaratta Base Hospital in Victoria's northeast where he was unconscious for three hours and treated for a depressed compound fracture of the skull. It took six weeks before doctors thought he was well enough to leave. However, not long after his discharge from hospital, Harry dived into a river and fractured his skull again. This time it took him a week to seek any medical treatment and, back in the same hospital, the doctors put a plate into his skull. Harry always said that apart from occasional headaches, he suffered no ill-effects from the two fractures; but Hazel always thought his injuries were why he giggled the whole time, and could have been the reason he didn't seem particularly smart.

Harry didn't go back to driving as a job and instead got work with the Country Roads Board of Victoria and, at the age of twenty-two, went back to live with his mother and stepfather who had made their home in the free camping area at Wangaratta.

Until then, Harry Bodsworth's life had been quite unremarkable. He had not been in any trouble, had no criminal convictions and not even in his wildest imagination could he have thought he would become a murderer. But in March 1950, his mum and stepfather had pitched their tent next to a woman with a sick husband and four children — Dulcie Baron. At five feet ten inches tall, with his fair hair and blue eyes, Harry soon caught Dulcie's eye.

*

Dulcie was forty-one and before she met Harry she had already lived a life and a half. She and Cavanagh had been so young when they married that she and Ted, or Old Ted as he became known, had grown up together. A rough diamond who liked a drink, he could be a real charmer. He wasn't a bad man and initially she thought he was fun as they made a living from seasonal work, picking peas or potatoes depending which was in season, sometimes just stealing them for food. Ted also trapped rabbits but unlike Harry, who sold them to factories, Ted set up by the side of the road and sold them for a few shillings.

Cavanagh and Dulcie never considered themselves out of work because they always scraped a living. Technology had arrived and the middle-class families started to invest in top-loading washing machines the size of cement mixers and new-fangled vacuum cleaners but Dulcie only saw such luxuries when she got work as a domestic in their homes. She picked up on what was happening around the world from the snippets she was able to read in the newspapers while working in shops but the growing talk of feminism passed her by. It was not because she wouldn't have supported it but she didn't have time to think about it. Dulcie always knew that women were superior to men and that they had to be even tougher to get on in life. If that meant using and abusing the men to do it, so be it. On top of that, she had four children before she was twenty-five.

She was still young, still attractive and kept herself clean and tidy but, unlike her, Old Ted had no ambitions to be anything else in life than a labourer living off the land and Dulcie was getting restless. In the late 1930s, before the outbreak of war, the family was living in a caravan in rural Wagga Wagga in New South Wales. There were the girls Hazel and Ruby, who was born in 1934, and the boys Edward, who was known as Billy, born May 1929 in the Goulburn Valley town of Tatura, and Ronnie, born in May 1933 in Violet Town in northeastern Victoria. Little is known about where Hazel and Ruby were born because their histories were lost as, along with their brothers, they were cast aside when Dulcie decided she was going to look for a better life. This time her escape route was Ted Baron, who had a proper house and whose parents had a farm. Dulcie took the kids and left Old Ted.

Years later Dulcie would tell the police that she had left the boys with their dad but that wasn't true. She had got to know a couple who ran a local general store, one of those that sold everything from fresh vegetables to nails and mops. They were in their forties and had never been able to have children. Dulcie conned them with a cock and bull story about having to go into hospital and have surgery and asked if they would look after Hazel Cavanagh for her until she was well again. Hazel was just nine months old and while the couple must have been suspicious, they didn't ask too many questions. Dulcie never went back and they brought Hazel Cavanagh up as their own daughter. Dulcie never told anyone the couple's names and Hazel Cavanagh probably never knew who her real parents were.

Ted Cavanagh had taught Dulcie to drive and, leaving the boys with a friend, Dulcie drove to a local orphanage. She walked in holding little Ruby's hand in hers and told the nuns the same story about needing surgery and asked would they look after her daughter. It was a common story in those days used by women who were too young or too poor to have children and who wanted a better life for them, but while the nuns had heard it all before, it was rare for them to see mothers in their twenties like Dulcie. They never turned anyone away and agreed to take Ruby in. Dulcie never returned and Ruby grew up in the orphanage where the nuns changed her name to Shirley Teresa. But she never forgot her real name — or her mother — and always preferred to be called Ruby. She also never forgot her surname was Cavanagh. It would be decades before she saw her mother again.

While Hazel and Ruby grew up alone, at least the boys had each other. Dulcie left them at an orphanage at Goulburn, using the same excuse of needing surgery. She kissed them goodbye and said she would be back for them but they never saw her again. They were only aged seven and three but the boys were like peas in a pod and kept in touch with each other their whole lives, dying within five weeks of each other. They never forgot 'Little Ruby' and tried to track her down but it took a long time before they found one another again.

Ted Cavanagh easily moved on from his wife leaving with his children although his family remembers him having one soft spot — his daughter Ruby. Like his two sons, he tried to look for her, but without knowing her new name of Shirley Teresa, he didn't have much luck. He also didn't know that she had met Gilbert McGloin while still at the orphanage and married him as soon as she left at the age of eighteen. McGloin was a local boy who had been courting Ruby while working as a storeman in Wagga Wagga since leaving the army in 1949.

Ted Cavanagh moved on with fifteen-year-old Greta and at her urging they moved to the now-trendy Sydney suburb of Paddington. In July 1941, he signed up for the army and became a driver, assigned to the General Duties Depot, and marched over 300 kilometres to the prisoner of war camp at Cowra.

Less than a month after joining the army, he was in hospital. Seven months later he was back in Sydney having reported sick or been in hospital no fewer than sixteen times with a number of complaints. During this time he contracted rheumatic fever. The autoimmune disease led to him developing serious heart problems which cut short his army career — but didn't stop him having nine children with Greta.

After some months in the new Yaralla Military Hospital on the banks of the Parramatta River in Concord, in March 1942 Ted Cavanagh was discharged medically unfit for service, his record showing it was 'not occasioned by his own default'. Less than eight months after he signed up, he was demobbed and moved his growing family to Colac in southwest Victoria.

The same big wet of the winter of 1950 that swelled the Murray River before Ted Baron died in its cold and muddy waters also flooded the Cavanagh family home on the shores of Lake Colac and they lost all their personal possessions. Five years later, Greta had to write to the army to get copies of her husband's discharge papers so he could go into a military hospital after he collapsed with heart problems.

'I'm truly desperate,' she wrote. 'My husband has completely collapsed and his heart mussels [sic] are gone and he is to be in hospital from three to nine months.'

The whole family was living in a caravan and only their oldest, at sixteen, had left home to fend for himself. Greta wrote that they also needed Ted's discharge papers to apply for his pension. With no fixed income, they were living on what she and one of their daughters could earn from pea picking which 'may terminate at any moment'. The army was happy to help and sent the family the papers they needed.

Like Dulcie's second husband, Ted Cavanagh would be an invalid for the rest of his life. Unlike Ted Baron, he had a loving and devoted wife to care for him.

*

With Ted Baron unable to work, their savings exhausted and no money for the rent, the Baron family had no choice but to pack up their belongings in a trailer, leave their lovely house in Beechworth and move forty kilometres down the road to the caravan at Wangaratta. Ted Baron was back in hospital with his worsening arthritis. Dulcie knew the reality of her life was once again as dull as dishwater but she would never let anyone know the truth. She liked to portray the image of a dedicated spouse, and people saw her as she wanted them to — a selfless wife, a caring mother. But she was sick of being married to a cripple, as she saw him.

Then, in 1950, along came Harry. Hazel always wondered what Harry saw in her mother, what with their age difference and the fact that Dulcie already had a family. Hazel could see, however, when she grew up and looked back, what had attracted her mother to Harry. He was young, good-looking and paid her compliments. Unlike her husband, he was vigorous. He wasn't a quick thinker but he was a good worker. And he was malleable; Dulcie could get him to believe almost anything. One of the popular pastimes at the camp was playing euchre, a trick-taking card game usually between four people in teams of two. Harry and Dulcie quickly paired up.

Whether Harry's mother and stepfather knew about the relationship, they said nothing. For Harry, the offer of not only sex but illicit, exciting, dangerous sex, was something not many hot-blooded 22-year-olds could turn down.

The Bible may have said that there was no rest for the wicked but Dulcie had always slept like a log. When Ted got home from one of his regular hospital visits, she suddenly developed 'insomnia'. She told him she couldn't get any rest, his snoring in the small caravan was keeping her awake and she desperately needed some peace and quiet. She told Ted she was off to try to sleep in their car, the big black Nash. She said she would take Hazel with her and the rest of the kids could have more space. To Hazel, she made it sound exciting and told her they were going camping, just the two of them. The truth was that it would have been too suspicious if she had gone off by herself. She told Hazel she would flog her if she ever told anyone what happened.

It was dark by 7 pm, Ted had taken his sleeping tablet and Dulcie had all the kids tucked up in bed. Once she started up the car and drove out of the camping ground, she turned left and pulled over to the verge, stopping just a couple of minutes along the road. Hazel wanted to know what was happening, why were they stopping by the side of the road? Dulcie told her to keep quiet. Then Hazel recognised the figure stepping out of the bushes and Harry climbed into the front seat. It was a spot just far enough away that no one in the camp ground could see them, not that Ted, with his arthritis, could have followed them. He could hardly move even when he hadn't taken his sleeping drug. Another fifteen minutes further on, Dulcie found a place where she could pull off the road into the bush and the car was hidden by trees. She made up a bed on the front seat with a pillow and blanket and Hazel had heaps of room to stretch out because her mother got into the back seat with Harry. It was the first of many nights that the rocking of the car sent her to sleep.

The next morning, they always stopped to let Harry out at the same spot where they had picked him up. 'Don't tell Dad that Harry was with us,' Dulcie admonished Hazel, the keeper of her secrets. 'Mind what you say or you will know about it.'

At the camping ground, Harry hovered around like a moth getting dangerously close to the flame. Not long after her forty-first birthday in July 1950, Dulcie started packing up and told the kids they were leaving. In the middle of it all, Ted Baron came home from hospital again, this time leaning on a walking stick for the first time. There was no confrontation, Ted wasn't like that, but the kids all stopped and stood by and watched as he asked Dulcie what she thought she was doing. Dulcie told him she was leaving.

Years later Hazel could cry when she recalled what happened next. Ted asked Dulcie if she was taking the children with her and she turned to the kids and, as young as they were, gave them an ultimatum — her or their dad. They knew their mum better than they knew their dad and first Hazel and then the others said they would go with her. Ted hung around awkwardly for a few days before he had to go back into hospital. While he was there, Dulcie finished packing, put the kids in the back of the car and with Harry — her future — in the front seat. They stopped when they got to Mildura because it seemed convenient and Dulcie wrote to Ted in hospital to tell them where the family was living. Ted hitched a lift to join them but ended up in Mildura Hospital.

*

After Ted Baron drowned and the inquest was over, Dulcie and Harry could stop pretending but their life was certainly no honeymoon. Dulcie sold the big army tents and they packed the rest of their meagre belongings in the trailer and took off. Just over a year after Ted's death, Dulcie and Harry married in Wangaratta in December 1951 and then moved back to Korumburra where their son was born a few months later, Dulcie's ninth child. Like Ted Baron, Harry had no idea of his wife's other family and first husband. The secrets were mounting up.

In Korumburra, the family rented rooms and for the few months they were in town, the kids rode to school on an old draught horse called Taffy. As the oldest, Hazel rode up the front, then came Allan, Margaret and Jim down the back. At school they jumped off in the order they had climbed on and let Taffy free in the paddock next to the school until home time.

Harry hadn't really thought through what it was going to be like living with five children and it was with great reluctance that he took on the role of stepfather as they lived a life on the run. Before they could put down roots in Korumburra, the family was up and moving, travelling from town to town across Victoria and South Australia, never staying anywhere for too long in case people got to know them. They were suspicious of everyone and kept changing their surname. One week they were Boyd, another they were Jones. Sometimes they used Harry's mother's new surname of Pill. Unemployment benefits had been available in Australia since 1945 but the Bodsworths never applied for the dole. They would have to both get an address and give it to the authorities and they would have had to be available and willing to work. Instead they relied on charities for food and clothing and money from odd-jobbing.

They were rarely in one place long enough for the children to go to school again and anyway, Dulcie didn't trust them talking to people when she wasn't there to keep them on track. Hazel and the others were belted by her if they spoke out of turn to anyone outside the family. Not in front of other people of course, as Dulcie never let reality get in the way of their image. She always had the kids as neatly dressed and as clean as possible. For much of the time, the kids had no idea who they were and what they were called. Often they forgot their new names. Was it Boyd or Jones this week? Whatever Harry had expected, it wasn't a reality like this and he got sick of dragging the children everywhere. Hazel heard her mother tell him more than once to placate him: 'They are our insurance. No one takes much notice of families. Just keep quiet.' Malleable as ever, that is just what he did.

If it was warm and dry, they slept under the stars, rolling out tarpaulins and their thin shearer's mattresses and getting under their waggas. When it was wet or cold, the car became their bedroom even though it was packed with all seven of them in it. Dulcie and Harry slept in the front seat where she was nursing the baby; the four siblings slept sitting up in the back where there was much jostling for position and arguing. 'Get off me.' 'Move over!'

They washed in public toilets and showered when they could at truck stops. If they spent a night or two in one spot, Dulcie got out a piece of rope which was strung between two trees as a washing line and she and Hazel hand-washed the clothes at a local toilet block.

In March 1952, they had to drive back to Korumburra where Dulcie stood before a court for the first time in her life. Under her married name of Hazel Dulcie Bodsworth, she was fined three pounds for the crime of imposition, or obtaining money by deception. She pleaded 'distress' and got off paying.

The best times were when Harry managed to secure work as a farm labourer. When they got lucky, they were allowed to make their home in the shearers' quarters. Sometimes they even got to live for a few weeks here and there in a house on a farm.

In 1953 they found themselves on a property just outside Naracoorte in South Australia, southeast of Adelaide on the way out to Mount Gambier. These kinds of jobs weren't advertised and they had pulled in down the dirt road of many farms seeking work only to be disappointed. This time, the couple running the farm said they had enough work to keep Harry busy for a month or two in return for a few shillings and accommodation. They took it. The month or two turned into over three months and the family made the shearers' quarters their home. There was plenty of work for Harry repairing fencing and the shearing pens as well as working on the land.

The quarters were rough and ready — a long low timber building with six separate bedrooms opening onto an open verandah. They could taste the dust inside the rooms as the wind blew through the gaps and under the doors and Hazel had her work cut out brushing the red dirt off the verandah every morning.

In the big kitchen at one end of the rooms there was a cast iron stove and a couple of tables. It may not have been much but to a family used to living out of their car, it was a palace. Dulcie and Harry took the biggest room and the kids threw their waggas on the beds in the other rooms, some of them with single beds, others with doubles which the twins shared so as not to sleep by themselves. They had never slept alone in their lives. Hazel took the room next to Dulcie and Harry. The kids could stretch out and sleep on the bunks and eat proper meals cooked by Dulcie. They were heartily sick of hot chip sandwiches. There were proper toilets and showers, which only had doors halfway up because they were usually used by men who had nothing to hide on the top. Hazel couldn't care less. Life was wonderful ... for a time.

For the kids there had been no room for wonder or curiosity in their lives as the minutiae of everyday survival dominated their time. Hazel was too busy subsisting, staying safe and trying to keep on her mother's good side. Hazel had taught the twins, then eight, how to read and write but they didn't have books of their own. Up at the big house, the couple's children were in their late teens and had a treasure trove of books, which the couple let Hazel borrow. One of her favourites was *Peter Pan*. It was a copy of the book in hardback with a pale blue cover, and out of its pages flew a dreamworld where children could take off to a life of adventure. She helped the twins read it, and for a few weeks their imaginations ran wild as they stood on their beds, closed their eyes and thought wonderful thoughts and waited for the fairy dust to sprinkle down on them with the gift of flight. But every time they stepped off the bed, their feet hit the ground.

One morning Hazel was woken before daylight. Harry threw open the door to her room and whispered loudly: 'Quick, your mum is sick. Come on.' He had a parcel wrapped in newspaper under his arm. Hazel raced to her mum's room. It was just coming on dawn and inside the room was dark. The only light was the dim bulb hanging from the ceiling and Hazel saw Dulcie lying on one of the single beds, her head on the pillow. Her face was pale, as white as a ghost, but the terrifying thing was that there was blood everywhere. The sheet covering Dulcie was red from her waist down. Hazel pulled the sheet back and screamed. She would never forget the sight she saw. There was a tiny baby between Dulcie's legs. It was a boy, she could see that, but it looked more like a skinned rabbit. And it wasn't breathing, just lying there.

Hazel ran out to tell Harry, who was digging a hole next to the clothes line and laying the newspaper parcel in it. Hazel could see that there was another tiny baby boy wrapped in the paper shroud.

Hazel was only thirteen but that morning she seemed to be the only grown-up. She told Harry to go up to the house and get them to ring for an ambulance. Harry grabbed her by the top of her left arm, gripping her until it hurt.

'Don't tell anyone about the babies, do you hear me? Loud and clear?' he said.

Hazel was shaking. 'No, I won't, I won't say anything, but there is another baby in the bed.'

Harry ran back inside the bedroom and came out with another newspaper parcel. He widened the hole and put the second baby into the sad little makeshift grave next to where the laundry was hung.

While Harry went to the house to use the telephone, Hazel stayed with her mum, holding her hand, as she thought Dulcie was going to die. Her mum had never looked so vulnerable. It was one of the few times that Dulcie couldn't berate her for something; she was so sick that she couldn't even speak. But even as she was comforting her mother, Hazel was angry at her for whatever had happened. She knew how babies were made by then — her own periods had started — and she knew this was not the right way to go about it. When the ambulance arrived, Allan was left to look after the kids and Harry and Hazel followed it to the hospital where Dulcie gave birth to two more stillborn babies and needed several blood transfusions.

A bank manager had recently moved to town and had put his name down as a blood donor. As it was a Sunday, he was playing tennis but he was dragged off the tennis courts to get to the hospital and make good his pledge to give blood. For Dulcie, it had been touch and go. The doctor told Harry that without the bank manager's blood, she would not have made it. There had been no time to wait for blood to come from Adelaide.

Once they knew Dulcie was going to pull through, the doctor told Harry he was so sorry. He said that Mrs Bodsworth would be fine but she had been about twenty-four weeks' pregnant, very late to have a miscarriage and especially tragic when there were quadruplets. The two he had seen were boys. The doctor said it looked as though she had already lost two babies before getting to hospital.

Hazel looked up, scared that they were going to get into trouble; the doctor seemed very stern. She saw Harry staring straight at her.

'I don't remember seeing any babies, doctor, only clots. Isn't that right, Aggie?' he said, using Hazel's pet name. All she could do was nod. Despite Harry's denials, it was recorded in state records that a mother had lost all her four quadruplets.

This time Dulcie had not shared her secret with Hazel — that she was pregnant again. She certainly hadn't looked like a pregnant woman and Hazel had not known any of the other signs to look for. Dulcie hadn't been to see a doctor although, as a serial mother, she would have known she was pregnant. It wasn't unusual in those days for women not to seek medical help until a month before they were due. But Dulcie had not even told Harry that they were going to have more children. Obviously she didn't know she was carrying quadruplets, but she didn't want even one more mouth to feed. Instead of doing something about it, Dulcie had ignored it. Even at forty-four she was still careless with her children. If they had survived they would have been her babies 10, 11, 12 and 13, all boys. Now two lay under the clothes line on the farm and two were in the incinerator at the hospital.

Hazel didn't know until years later, but Dulcie put a death notice in one of the major Victorian papers announcing her own end so that Ted Baron's relatives wouldn't come looking for her. Despite that, Hazel's grandmother, Agnes Baron, never stopped looking for the children until she died in 1960.

CHAPTER THREE

SAM OVERTON

THE ORANGE DUST WAS KICKING UP ACROSS THE DRY SHEEPLANDS of Netallie Station the afternoon Dulcie decided to pick an argument with the cook. Tom never stood a chance after the Bodsworths arrived and Dulcie had decided she wanted his job along with the access it gave to his boss, station manager Milton Samuel Overton, known as Sam.

Tom was an English bloke and, as such, good at cooking hearty farm fare like meat and three veg. There was always plenty of mutton to turn into a meal on a sheep station. He wasn't into fancy cuisine like cooking with wine but he certainly liked to drink the stuff. Tom lived alone in a room in one of the sheds on the hill behind the main house where the wine and a tot or four of whisky helped him cope with loneliness. As the housekeeper, Dulcie was the only other regular worker in the main house and she could smell the alcohol on Tom's breath every day but she just bided her time until events gave her the chance she was looking for.

Tom had been at Netallie for some weeks before Overton took over as station manager in October 1955, two months before

Dulcie and her family blew in on a foul wind. As his drinking got worse, so did his timekeeping and Overton, although not a stickler for punctuality, liked his tea on the table at five every day. In the cities, they would have called it dinner but in the bush, it was always tea, a cooked tea of course, not a 'city' afternoon tea of cakes and scones. Tom's increasing tardiness did not go unnoticed by Dulcie but she made it a point never to help him if the meals were late. He could dig his own grave, she thought.

Whether it was true or not, Dulcie took it upon herself this scorching afternoon in December 1955 to tell the hapless cook that the boss had had enough. She said Overton had asked her to tell Tom that he was sacked.

The language in the kitchen was as hot as the wind blowing outside. Young Jim was listening by the door as his mother ordered Tom out of the kitchen and off the station while in his flat English accent, Tom told her she was a bitch. And a bullying bitch at that. Dulcie was standing by the stove where she had a saucepan of water boiling on the hob. She picked up the pan while shouting at Tom that she would scald him for life if he didn't do what she said and get out of her road, right now. Tom knew he had lost the argument and, with a final expletive, he turned and ran away in his singlet and working pants with Dulcie following him to the kitchen door. She lifted her right hand and threw the boiling water at him, leaving a red scald mark down the right side of his back; it took days to go away.

Her last words to him hung in the air as he fled her attack: 'It does not do to cross me.'

Another local farming family had already discovered the truth of that statement.

Before the Bodsworths landed at Netallie, they had worked at Burragan Station, a nearby property; that is, 'nearby' by country standards. While Netallie is sixteen kilometres west of the town of Wilcannia, the turn-off to Burragan is ninety kilometres east of the town back along the Barrier Highway and then another twenty-seven kilometres down a dirt road.

When the Bodsworths pulled into town in their big black Nash car in May 1955, Wilcannia was like the big smoke to the kids. Even though the town was just a shadow of its former self, the grand buildings from its glory days when it was known as the 'Queen City of the West' still looked imposing. Along the shore of the Darling River between the red gums, the beautiful old sandstone warehouses that used to be filled by the busy paddle steamers plying their trade seventy years earlier were empty but had not then fallen into disrepair. It was no longer the third largest port in New South Wales after Sydney and Newcastle but it was still at the heart of a vast farming district with a thriving community and a famous store, Knox and Downs, where it was said you could buy everything from a boiled lolly to a windmill.

Even better was that no one in Wilcannia knew the Bodsworths, which was why Dulcie figured it was as good as anywhere to stop for a while. They set up in the campsite along the river where they managed to find a large tent and Harry asked around for work. Dulcie felt so comfortable that the children were even allowed to use their real names.

Hazel was still only fifteen but Dulcie had put her age up two years, and she had been working as a domestic to supplement the family's meagre income as they travelled from town to town. She certainly felt and acted older than she was so it was easy for her to pass as seventeen. All the kids had to grow up pretty quickly because of their way of life. There had been no time for Hazel to play with dolls; instead, she had moved on to the real thing — looking after her brothers and sister. Dulcie treated her like a grown-up and told Hazel that she had to go and get herself some work if they were going to stay in Wilcannia a while. About the same time as Harry heard that they might need some help at Burragan, Hazel got her first real job — as a nurse's aide at the local hospital. She hadn't done any nursing before but walked up to the front door, told them she was seventeen and asked if they had any work. To her amazement, they asked her how soon she could start. It was the turning point in Hazel's life that made her the woman she became.

The hospital was a beautiful colonial sandstone building along the river, fronting onto Ross Street. It was a magnificent example of early Australian architecture with wide verandahs shading it from the heat before there was any air conditioning. Nurse's aides started in the pan room, literally: they cleaned up the shit. Hazel loved it because the aides also got to do everything the nurses did except for actually treating the patients, giving injections or handing out drugs. It had less than thirty beds but Wilcannia Hospital then operated like a general hospital. It had a maternity ward and there were operating theatres, although it had only one full-time doctor, the local general practitioner Dr John Louis Potts who was also the hospital's medical superintendent. Other doctors were brought in when needed by the Royal Flying Doctor Service.

Hazel's uniform was a blue dress with buttons up the front, fitted at the waist with a white apron over it and she didn't even have to press it because their laundry was done for them. On her head she wore a blue cap with a band around it.

The best thing was that she moved away from Dulcie's watchful eye. In the Nurses' Homestead, she had her own bedroom, and there were clean bathrooms, a sitting room and a big table where they all ate their meals, which were cooked for them. Hazel felt she had stepped through a door into another world. The rules were strict but she took to them more easily than some of the other nurse's aides — after all, they hadn't been brought up with Dulcie as their mother. Matron lived in the nurses' quarters as well and no one could begin to eat until she had sat at the table and said grace. Those were the days when matrons were looked on with awe and expected to be treated like the Queen, which the Wilcannia matron certainly was.

However, Dulcie soon realised that by telling Hazel to get a job, she had relinquished some of her control over her daughter. To regain some of it, she made Hazel give her five pounds from the six pounds she was paid every fortnight. Arguing with Dulcie about it would have been a waste of time for Hazel. Hazel loved her job and she knew that if she didn't agree to hand over most of her wages, Dulcie would cause trouble and ruin everything for her.

But Hazel had made the first move, however small, to break away from the power exerted by her mother.

*

Burragan Station was not the easiest place to find. Margaret Fitzgerald, known as Madge, and her only daughter Elinor, known as Lin, were such fiercely independent and private people that they even had their mailbox set up on the opposite side of the highway from the driveway to their property. At one stage, it was positioned many kilometres away from the entrance. What few visitors there were rarely got past the woolshed, about halfway between the start of the dirt road and the homestead. Those who did make it were treated to the sight of a magnificent garden with fruit trees and, at the right time of year, a passionfruit vine laden with fruit growing over trellises between two splendid kurrajong trees. Invariably the visitors would comment on how much they loved passionfruit.

'That's nice,' old Madge would say but never offer them any, even as her fruit lay rotting on the ground.

Mother and daughter had no option but to take on help after Madge's husband, Des, died in 1948. Des Fitzgerald had owned parts of the sheep and cattle station since 1903 and by his death, the family owned 70,000 acres. His demise brought Lin home from boarding school in Adelaide aged fifteen, where she took to working on the land harder than any man, out there from sunup to sundown 365 days of the year. She mustered sheep, hauled them on their backs to crutch them, hoisted 44-gallon drums full of fuel onto the back of utes and kept the bores clear for fresh water. Her mother, then in her seventies, always kept a frugal house, wearing an apron made from hessian sugar bags tied around her waist.

As the formidable widow and her daughter struggled to maintain Burragan, it would often be weeks before they would get into town, about an hour's drive away, and the two of them became even more secluded. They had a couple of station hands, including Laurie (who Lin married in 1964 much to her mother's disapproval because he then saw it as his right never to work again), and in 1955, took on Harry Bodsworth and his stepson Allan, then fourteen and strong enough to work on the land.

The family moved into the two-bedroom cottage next to the homestead, with the twins and their half-brother living with Harry and Dulcie, and Allan living in the shearers' quarters about four kilometres away. Dulcie rarely called Jim and Margaret by their names; they were invariably 'the twins', as in: 'Twins, get the washing up done.' Old Madge only needed the muscle the men brought but she thought Dulcie might as well do some housework and cooking. The main house wasn't grand but it was solid and filled with old colonial furniture, some of it antique like the carved round table with spindle-back chairs. There were brass beds, meat safes and the then-obligatory treadle sewing machine. They didn't have a washing machine and the laundry was still done in tubs.

There was much more room in the homestead than in the cottage and Dulcie couldn't see why she shouldn't take it over. Why should old Madge have it when she had only the one daughter while the Bodsworths were a young family? It wasn't fair. Dulcie had tried to ingratiate herself with Madge but while her act worked with men, the women could always see through her. Madge was on to her quick smart. Madge was not the friendliest of people anyway and she dealt with Dulcie by keeping her at arm's-length, polite but very firm. Madge was nothing if not direct and she couldn't abide people who were two-faced. She knew that Dulcie had been bad-mouthing her behind her back but pretending to be nice to her face. She had no idea how dangerous the woman could be if she perceived she had been slighted.

Dulcie's thoughts became a plan, which she put into action. She thought if the mother and daughter had enough bad luck, they would move into town, leaving her and Harry to look after Burragan.

She started to talk about how the owners were 'too big for their boots' and treated her badly, even if she was convincing no one but herself. Hazel had bought a pushbike which she was paying off at ten shillings a fortnight but it was too far to cycle out to Burragan so the only times she visited were when Harry or Dulcie picked her up and gave her a lift. On one visit, Allan told Hazel that their mother had said the two Fitzgerald women should really move into town and then she could live in the homestead and manage the property. He told her how Dulcie had already staged a couple of accidents by making one of the rainwater tanks spring a leak. On another occasion, the forever malleable Harry had taken a part out of the engine in the truck so it wouldn't start for Lin Fitzgerald.

Hazel knew that it was pie in the sky stuff for Dulcie to imagine the Fitzgeralds would move.

'It's never going to happen,' she told Allan. 'They have grown onto the buildings and this is their life. They are part of their farm.'

She noted Allan's concerns but although it sounded ominous, Hazel was too excited with her new life to take the warnings very seriously and she didn't think anything really bad would happen. She didn't want to say anything to Dulcie because she knew she would get belted. So she left Dulcie the five pounds for that fortnight and went back to the nurses' quarters and her new friend Connie Paterson, who had moved up from Adelaide as a registered nurse.

The woolshed got it first. Dulcie chose a day when all the station hands were out in their trucks and utes, and on 7 October 1955, she got Allan to drive her to the woolshed where she poured a mixture of sugar and kerosene onto the bales of wool and set them on fire. She knew she could rely on Allan to keep his mouth shut as he was too terrified of her to speak up. They drove back to the main house before the blaze was discovered. By the time the others smelt the fire and followed the smoke back to the woolshed, it had been destroyed. Dulcie could not have been more sympathetic to the Fitzgeralds. What a terrible thing to happen! Madge had the police come and investigate but there was nothing left of the shed and it was put down to an accident, perhaps a cigarette butt, although no one admitted to having been smoking near there.

The only heating in the homestead was from fireplaces in two of the rooms and the cooking was done on a wood-fired stove. A few weeks later, on 3 December, Dulcie started a fire in the wood heap next to the main house and it burnt the whole place to the ground. (Luckily it was before the Fitzgeralds started to hide their fortune in the house, after it was rebuilt. When Lin died in a nursing home in Broken Hill in 2011, hundreds of thousands of dollars were found hidden under floorboards, in the back of cupboards and wrapped in the pages of newspapers.)

Dulcie had met her match in Madge Fitzgerald. Madge had again called the local Wilcannia police and fire brigade and while there was no evidence, she was sure Dulcie was behind both the house fire and the blaze at the woolshed. After watching everything she owned go up in flames, she gave Dulcie and Harry their marching orders, told them to pack up and get out. The family once again put their shearer's mattresses and the waggas in the trailer and got into the Nash. Taking the wheel, Dulcie drove to the highway, shaking Burragan off like the dust from the car's wheels.

Sam Overton was to prove a much easier target for Dulcie. Not even the bush telegraph could have put him on alert because the Fitzgeralds kept themselves to themselves. They weren't on the radar.

As the Bodsworths moved to the other side of Wilcannia and onto the 60,000-acre Netallie Station, Hazel was finding out what it was like to have friends for the first time in her life. She had never had other kids to play with, just her brothers and sister, and it was fun to go out to the tearooms in Wilcannia or organise a picnic on the banks of the Darling River on a day off. Her best friend Connie — Sister Paterson to the patients — had moved to Wilcannia for love. She had met Robert Knox in her home town of Adelaide and followed him to the bush where his family owned the Knox and Downs store. He was something of a catch with his wealth and prestige, a bit like the James Packer of Wilcannia. He had taken over from his father, also called Robert Knox, as the chairman of the Knox and Downs company after Mr Knox senior died in 1948. The pioneering family had played a major role in opening up the White Cliffs opal fields and were also into shipping.

Hazel always thought them a strange match because Connie was tall, elegant and beautiful while Robert was quite dumpy and turning to fat, but they were in love. Connie was staying at the Nurses' Homestead until they got married.

At Netallie Station, Sam Overton was managing it for his wife's family, the McClures, a farming dynasty who had owned it since 1917. It already had its own little spot in history as Constance Desailly, the daughter of a previous owner, had married Edward Dickens, known as Plorn to friends and family. Along with his older brother, Plorn had been encouraged to migrate to Australia by their father, the great novelist Charles Dickens. The man who gave the world Oliver Twist and Ebenezer Scrooge thought his sons would have a better life away from the filthy cities of industrial England. Constance became Mrs Dickens in 1880 and the couple held their wedding reception at Netallie Station while her husband went on to become the local MP.

Overton used to have a property of his own, called 'Ellameek', at Frances in the southeast of South Australia, coincidentally not far from Naracoorte, where Dulcie had lost her last four babies. His wife, Margaret McClure, worked as a nurse in Adelaide and usually visited at Christmas and Easter, bringing with her their son David during the school holidays. The McClures were part of Adelaide society and when the couple married in November 1939, it made it into the social pages of South Australia's *The Advertiser*, her dark hair under a white veil and him looking dashing with his thin moustache on top of a wide, smiling mouth. For no reason at all other than jealousy, Dulcie took an instant dislike to Margaret Overton. Not that she ever let Margaret know her true feelings.

The mid-1950s were boom years for Australia's wool industry and the magnificent prices made farmers happy for a change. The

McClures had done as well as the other families living off the sheep's back and invested in large homes in the middle of Adelaide and in the Adelaide Hills. Margaret was one of a very close family of three brothers and four sisters and one of her nieces, Miss South Australia Julianna McClure, married Squadron Leader Kym Bonython, part of the Bonython family who were even higher up the social scale than the McClures and were like royalty in South Australia. Kym, the youngest child of Sir John Lavington Bonython, had been awarded the Distinguished Flying Cross in World War II and would go on to welcome (as the promoter's representative) the Beatles to Adelaide in 1964.

These were the people Overton had socialised with as he lived in Adelaide for a few years after selling Ellameek and moving to Netallie Station, so he had accumulated a good city wardrobe, which he had brought with him. He was noted as one of the best-dressed men in the area. While the station hands and other station owners dressed like drovers in the dust, Overton wore the best riding boots and liked each pair to be kept polished. Hanging up in his bedroom, he had neatly pressed slacks, trousers, two good suits and three tweed sports coats. He was a strong, tall man at about five feet ten inches, who weighed about thirteen stone, had brown hair and was at the peak of good health. Actually, Dulcie realised, he was about the same size and build as Harry. When she polished the boots, she even checked their size — a 10, just like Harry. She thought Overton's clothes would look even better on her husband, especially those sports coats. She could picture Harry in them.

Harry was working as the overseer on the property in the summer of 1955 and early 1956 when the temperatures soared to forty or fifty degrees in the day and drought was a constant companion. Once again the family had fallen on their feet and they lived in a stone cottage about fifty metres to the north of the rambling homestead. Every morning Harry walked to the main house to get his orders for the day from Overton. On a good day, Netallie was the most beautiful place in the world, the flat lands going on forever as if they were falling off the ends of the earth. But it was harsh land, the ground as hard as the hobs of hell, trodden solid by the hooves of the sheep. The day Dulcie chased Tom the cook out of the kitchen was the day he handed in his notice. While Harry was in control outside, Dulcie now had control inside the house. She was cook as well as housekeeper. And her heart was as barren as the land.

Dulcie never dwelt on the past, as evidenced by the fact the only person she told about her secret family was Hazel. She had never gone looking for her first four children. She had never spoken about the shocking births at Naracoorte, which almost took her life. Ted Baron was as lost to her as those dead babies — unless she needed him, when she would roll him out like a prop in a play. Now that she had Sam's ear at the dining table, she launched into her hard-luck stories, the ones that worked so well on men. She was a widow, had loved her husband and it had been a shock when he died. They had done it tough but how lucky was the family when Harry came along. Sam was sucked in. They got on well and became friends, because Dulcie could be witty and entertaining. But she never became too familiar or put a foot above what she knew was her station. That would never have done. She knew she needed Sam on side. To everyone, including him, she was always Mrs Bodsworth. To her, he was always Mr Overton. He thought she was an excellent cook, certainly better than Tom, with the tea on the table by five on the dot. She always did him proud at breakfast with his favourite — lamb chops with eggs and thick gravy.

Everyone in the bush could shoot; and after Mrs Overton and David had left in January 1956 to return to Adelaide following their Christmas holiday, Sam took up his favourite sport again. He called on Dr Potts, who'd been in town only for as long as Overton had, and the local parish priest, both single men, and they would ride out on the property to shoot ducks. The three men enjoyed each other's company, a drink and the food served up by Dulcie when they got back. Sometimes they would take Allan along with them and he spoke about it as some of the best times he ever had.

One day as the shooting party was leaving, Dulcie took Allan aside: 'Allan, while youse are out shooting, could you accidentally shoot Sam on the other side of the swamp?'

Allan thought she was joking and didn't take it seriously but when the men all came back safe that afternoon, Dulcie said: 'Well, at least you could have done it, Allan.' He thought she sounded a bit put out.

Netallie Station was close enough to Wilcannia for Hazel to cycle there and every fortnight she rode out to give Dulcie her wages. Allan told her during one visit how much he loved going out shooting with the men. He also confided in her about their mother's comment regarding shooting Sam. Like him, Hazel was not sure if it had been a joke.

Hazel had never met Mrs Overton but she wasn't surprised that Dulcie didn't like her. Allan told her about one conversation he had had with Dulcie. She told him: 'If Sam wasn't here, that woman wouldn't be visiting and we would take over. Harry would have the manager's job and we would be in the main house instead of being stuck in the shearers' quarters.'

Even Hazel had no idea how far her mother would go this time.

*

Meanwhile, Hazel had fallen in love; or rather, she had fallen in comfort. Love was to come later but come it did and last the rest of her life.

The patient in the bed in the corner of the men's ward at Wilcannia Hospital had been admitted to have his appendix out. Bill was aged twenty, one of a family of twelve siblings, and his family owned 65,000 acres at White Cliffs west of Wilcannia. Hazel was drawn to him because he was such a gentle man, which was even better than a gentleman — although he was one of those as well. He was a truly gentle soul. Just what she needed. That he was young and handsome also helped.

Hazel was a bit bossy, as a good nurse's aide had to be, but she found herself fussing about Bill more than her other patients. She made sure she kept him cool by hanging wet towels over the fan in his ward. Hazel was fifteen and didn't know what love was, but Bill was in hospital for six weeks and had enough time to start to court her. Hazel thought she was ugly — tall, skinny, with freckles and curly hair. No one had ever told her she looked beautiful but a beautiful young woman is what Bill saw when he looked at her. He was her first boyfriend and she was his first girlfriend. When he was discharged from hospital and went back to his parents' station, they wrote to each other and Hazel confided in Connie that she really liked him. She even told Dulcie because she knew she would find out anyway. Dulcie told Hazel there might be a vacancy coming up on Netallie which Bill could have, saying: 'Sam probably won't be here for very long.'

Dulcie, Harry, Allan and the kids were the only ones, apart from Overton, living on Netallie until shearer Daniel English arrived with his team of men on 10 April 1956, to help with the crutching. The shearing sheds and the sheep dip were close to the shearers' quarters, about fourteen and a half kilometres from the homestead. After the sheep had the wool cut from around their tail and between their rear legs, they were plunged into a wooden sheep dip filled with water mixed with arsenic, which killed the lice and protected against the blowflies which like to lay their eggs in the moist area under the sheep's tail. The poison was something you couldn't play around with and Overton made sure the station hands knew that. Even the dogs were kept clear when the sheep were being dipped. On Netallie they used a white powder product called Calarsenite, which contained about fifty per cent arsenic.

Dulcie had never heard of Calarsenite before she moved to Netallie but now she knew where to find it. The powder was kept in packets in boxes inside a wooden crate with the name 'Elliott's Calarsenite' written on the side and the initials of the town supplied stamped next to it: 'K and D Wilcannia', Knox and Downs. The crate was on the shelves among the tins and boxes inside the skin shed, which was used for storing chemicals and the skins of sheep that had been slaughtered. Dulcie took a cup full of the powder up to the house.

That Saturday, 14 April, Daniel took Overton into Wilcannia in the Jeep to pick up some supplies but when he called around to the main house the next day to take him up to the shearing sheds, he found the boss in agony. 'I'll lay down for a while. I'll go up when it cools off. I've never felt like this before,' Overton told him.

He felt so sick that he said: 'A man would be better off dead.'

Three days later, Hazel was on duty on 17 April when Sam Overton was admitted to Wilcannia Hospital, looking as sick as a dog. He hadn't even wanted to wait for an ambulance and Allan and Harry helped him into the back of a ute where he lay on a mattress as Harry drove him to town. He was taken down from the ute and carried into the hospital and put into bed. He was conscious but he couldn't sit up. Dr Potts was called and Hazel and the nurses tried to make the patient as comfortable as possible.

The doctor, Overton's shooting companion, had been out to see him at Wilcannia the previous day after he was telephoned by Dulcie. When he had arrived, she had her 'work face' on, the mask full of sympathy and concern but with a bit of a bite. Overton was in bed and before she took Dr Potts to see him, she drew him aside and spoke of her worry that her boss had been drinking too much. She had found empty wine and beer bottles; and also, he hadn't been eating and he had lost weight. He had been neglecting himself, she said, and she had been doing her best to try to help him.

Dr Potts found his friend as sick as he had ever seen anyone. The last time he had seen him was just a couple of weeks earlier and Overton had been his usual fit and healthy self. He tried to persuade Overton that hospital was the best place for him but the man was stubborn. He was sweating and told the doctor he had never felt so crook in his life. He had taken sick soon after crutching and it had only got worse. According to his notes, which he would come to rely on in a few years' time, Dr Potts diagnosed acute gastroenteritis and gave him an injection of Chloromycetin, a broad-based antibiotic, which was meant to knock the problem on the head. On the dresser in the bedroom, he left some capsules of a sedative, an antacid tablet and some vitamin tablets, which he told Dulcie she could administer over the next couple of days if they were needed.

But that next day when he saw Overton in hospital, Dr Potts became really worried. He immediately started intravenous infusion, inserting the catheter through Overton's leg. Overton was sweating profusely, his blood pressure had plummeted and he was in what the doctor called a 'moderately shocked' condition. He had developed severe diarrhoea, and was vomiting and convulsing.

His wife was notified in Adelaide and she immediately set off to be with him. Overton was placed in a private room for his own comfort and in case he had anything that might be contagious.

After she ended her shift that evening, Hazel went to see Overton. She pulled up the chair next to his bed and spoke words of comfort to him, telling him he would be fine. He looked up from the pillow and said: 'Hazel, your mother is so kind to me. You are lucky to have her.'

A shiver went through her and the hairs on her arms stood up. In her room at the nurses' quarters, Hazel didn't sleep that night. She didn't know what her mother had done but she feared her hand was behind this somehow.

When Hazel reported for duty the next morning, she learnt that Dr Potts had been called at 4.30 am when Overton had tried to get out of bed and had collapsed on the floor. The hospital notes showed the doctor injected him with the stimulant nikethamide, known then by its trade name Coramine, to get his heart rate up. He was put on oxygen and given other treatments. The nurses had him under 24-hour observation and Dr Potts was in and out of his room all day. Overton seemed to improve somewhat and Mrs Overton arrived at the hospital about 9 pm, having driven nonstop from Adelaide because there were no flights available at the right time. Hazel clocked off duty feeling more positive.

When she got back the next morning, she headed for Overton's room to see how he was but Connie Paterson grabbed her arm and stopped her from going in. The registered nurse said he had died during the night. He had collapsed suddenly at 10.45 pm and despite Dr Potts being called, Overton had died soon after. He was forty-two. Mrs Overton had been taken back to Netallie Station and some of her relatives were on their way from Adelaide to be with her.

Hazel felt numb. She was desperate to see her brother Allan because while she didn't want to believe it, she just knew her mother had got away with another murder. She was seething but also questioned herself: was there anything she could have done to stop it and save Overton's life? She felt sick. It was an awful predicament to be in at the age of fifteen.

There was no autopsy because Dr Potts was sure that Overton had died of natural causes and on the death certificate, he recorded two reasons — toxic myocarditis, which is an inflammation of the myocardium, the middle layer of the heart wall, and which reduces the heart's ability to pump blood around the body, and acute gastroenteritis. There was nothing suspicious about Overton's death at the time to merit the coroner getting involved, and the law was that the coroner was not automatically notified because Overton had seen a doctor shortly before his death. No one was looking for anyone to blame.

It was two days before Allan could get a lift into Wilcannia to talk to Hazel. They went through all the hints Dulcie had given that she had something bad on her mind. She had told Allan to see if he could 'accidentally' shoot Sam. Then there were the comments that Sam wasn't going to be around for long. It was all stuff they could put down to their mother thinking she could rule the roost again. But there was something else Allan had to tell his big sister.

During the first days that Overton was sick, Allan had walked into the kitchen and seen Dulcie preparing what she said was Sam's 'medicine'.

'It was some capsules that were open on the sink,' he told his big sister. 'She had them spread apart on the sink on some paper and I asked what they were.'

Allan paused as if not wanting to know the answer himself.

'She said that Sam wouldn't eat and they had to feed him through the capsules,' he said.

Hazel wanted to know what Dulcie was putting into the capsules but all Allan knew was that it was a white powder which he thought looked like powdered milk.

It was some days before Dr Potts had been called out to see Overton but at the time Allan hadn't thought too much about it. Now he told Hazel that it may have been Calarsenite. In the light of Overton's death, it was a chilling observation. They feared Dulcie may have poisoned him. Neither of them needed to remind the other that their mother had already killed once: their father.

They were sure she was responsible but they discussed the fact that they had no evidence to go to the police with, just a gut feeling. No one who had seen Dulcie with her mask on would have believed them. Everyone liked her. The brother and sister were scared of what Dulcie would do if they spoke up, especially Allan who was still living with his mother and stepfather. They even feared that she might poison Allan. Beneath the pleasant façade, she was a harsh, tough and cruel woman.

Meanwhile, Overton's body had been released for burial and was on its way to Adelaide by train via Broken Hill in a sealed zinc-lined casket. There was no refrigeration in those days so a zinc coffin was the only way to move bodies long distance, even though it made the caskets heavy and costly to freight.

Hazel and Allan thought they were alone in suspecting foul play; if only they had known that the McClure family also 'smelled a rat', as they would later describe it. Dulcie was furious when back at Netallie Station the day after her husband died, Margaret Overton outright accused her of poisoning him. She said he had never been sick in his life and that Dulcie must have known what had happened. Why hadn't Dulcie called her as soon as he became ill? Dulcie remained outwardly calm as she told Mrs Overton that she understood she was distressed but denied having anything to do with her husband's death. She then went outside and told Harry to drive her into town to Wilcannia police station.

Dulcie thought she would get one up on Mrs Overton, cut her off in her tracks. On her way out, Dulcie picked up a bottle of powder with a purple label from the kitchen. When she entered the police station she handed it over the counter to Sergeant Fred Marshall.

'I found this poison in the office at Netallie Station. I would like you to take it as I am afraid some of my children might get poisoned,' she told the officer, concern washing over her face. He told her that it looked like strychnine. She said she was shocked, and pleased she had taken it to the police.

When Dulcie and Harry got back to Netallie, they found that Mrs Overton had left to accompany her husband's body to Adelaide. Two of her brothers, Jim and Lance McClure, arrived at Netallie on 21 April to take charge. Margaret had told them what she thought of Dulcie, and the brothers decided to tread lightly.

Jim McClure went into the bedroom to look at Overton's personal effects and couldn't find his best shoes or any riding boots. The good slacks Overton liked to wear had also gone. Overton had always carried a fair bit of cash with him but there was no money in his wallet. He asked Dulcie where the clothing had gone and she said nothing was missing as far as she knew.

'These here are the only ones I noticed,' she said.

Then she started fingering the sports coats.

'Do you think Mrs Overton would let me have these sports coats? I feel they would fit my husband,' she asked him.

He knew what his sister would think — over her dead body. 'Oh no, I don't think so, Mrs Bodsworth,' he told her.

Dulcie continued to try to put the blame onto Overton for his own death. She told the brothers that he had been drinking heavily before he got sick and that the alcohol may have had something to do with his illness. Jim and Lance knew Overton liked a drink at a party and perhaps at a hotel on a Saturday afternoon but he never drank at home and could hardly be considered a heavy drinker.

Dulcie had them follow her to the dining room off the kitchen where she opened a cupboard and waved her right hand in triumph, indicating Overton's 'stash'. There was a total of four empty beer bottles and two empty wine bottles. The brothers scoffed.

'Even if a man drank all that, all in one day, he wouldn't be sick for more than a day or two at the most, so it couldn't have been the drinking,' Jim said.

Dulcie did not like being outsmarted.

The next morning, Harry walked over from the cottage to see what the brothers wanted him to do. They thought Harry seemed a bit simple and that he might tell them the truth so they engaged him in conversation about what had happened to Overton.

Then they heard a yell from the cottage and looked up to see Mrs Bodsworth at the door holding a shotgun. They knew enough about guns to know that they were too far away to be hurt but she was pointing it in their direction and seemed pretty bloody intimidating all the same.

'Get away from them, Harry, get away from them,' she shouted as she waved the gun around. Her husband appeared more afraid of his wife than the brothers were.

They called the police and Sergeant Marshall was one of the two officers who came from Wilcannia. There were only three officers stationed in the town and one of them was on a day off, so it was more or less their full strength. The officers disappeared into the cottage for about thirty minutes and when they finally emerged, the brothers could hear the officers thanking Dulcie for the tea and scones.

The brothers asked if the officers had taken the gun off her.

'No, no, she's just a bit upset,' Sergeant Marshall said. 'She's a good woman; no need to worry about her.'

What may have passed for 'upset' in Wilcannia was not what they ever wanted to see again and the brothers told Dulcie and Harry to leave. The couple dragged out their departure, borrowing a truck to move their furniture into town where Dulcie left the key in the ignition and the engine running when they brought it back so the battery would run down — just out of spite.

The McClures also discovered nails had been hammered into the rainwater tanks, as Dulcie had decided to 'bugger their lives up' before she left. The next generation of McClure children who holidayed at Netallie would be told tales of Mrs Bodsworth. She became like a bogeyman, or rather bogeywoman. They called the deserted cottage where she had lived 'Bodsworthville' and scared each other so much that they were too terrified to open the door and venture inside.

CHAPTER FOUR

TOMMY TREGENZA

TWO THOUSAND POUNDS. AS SOON AS DULCIE HEARD TOMMY Tregenza saying he had two thousand pounds in the bank, the town drunk suddenly morphed into someone who needed a friend like Dulcie Bodsworth.

Thomas Tregenza had a little ditty he liked to repeat: 'By Tre, Pol and Pen, you shall know the Cornishmen.' It was a version of an old rhyming couplet about the unique prefixes that were an integral part of place names and surnames in Cornwall. Tommy, as he was known, was very proud of his heritage and told people his descendants had come from Cornwall as part of the convict muster. They may well have, but Tregenza was born in Naracoorte in May 1887. In the early decades of the 1900s, the town barely had a population of 1500. Dulcie had left four dead babies there, two of them buried under a clothes line. She was also suspected by some people of killing Sam Overton, who had owned a farm there. If Tregenza had known about the curse of Naracoorte, he would have done well to stay clear of Mrs Bodsworth.

As well as his Cornish heritage, he was proud of what he had achieved in his own past even though he lived from hand to mouth in the present and had long ago written off the future.

His only real luck in life was his size: Tregenza was just over five feet in the old measurement and had always been wiry in build. He was the ideal size and shape to be a jockey and he loved horses, admiring their intelligence and beauty. He began his career in the saddle as an apprentice with one of the local stables. It was at the time when Australians were experimenting with the riding style where the jockeys crouched on short stirrups and Tregenza found it made racing easier. He was a natural. He raced in Victoria and New South Wales as well as South Australia. He never raced in the Adelaide Cup but at the same time, he never had a 'run-of-the-mill' victory — every time he was first past the post seemed like the first time. He revelled in the adoration of the crowd when he rode a winner. He wasn't famous but every time he won, he was a minor celebrity. In the so-called sport of kings, he felt like a king.

The end of their heyday would have destroyed a lot of people but Tregenza knew he had brought about his downfall himself. The demon drink. He was a demon who lived to drink. He drank to celebrate a win and drank to commiserate with himself when he didn't.

'Tre' in the Cornish language means a settlement or homestead but it was only in his name that Tregenza had either. After he quit as a jockey, he drifted around the three states, working as a miner at the Mount Drysdale gold mine near Cobar in New South Wales, as a drover or as a shearer. He had even worked at Netallie as a station hand before the Bodsworths arrived there.

His passions in life were drinking, smoking — and pea soup. In that order. His alcohol consumption led to a few run-ins with the law. In 1946, he had been 'admonished' and fined thirty shillings in Hay Magistrates Court after pleading guilty to the charges of drunkenness and using 'indecent language'. Court records show he had been droving cattle down south and was on his way back north with his pay packet when he was found worse for wear on the Balranald Road after getting drunk on red wine. Tired of hearing him swearing loudly, which was disturbing his wife and family, a householder called the police and Tregenza ended up in the dock the next morning after sobering up overnight in the police cells. He paid his fine and moved on.

*

After being kicked off Netallie Station, the Bodsworths moved back to Wilcannia where, despite the rumours that followed them both from Netallie and from Burragan Station, people were still willing to give Dulcie a go. It could be said that she cooked her way into their hearts. Stanley Davis employed her in the position he called cook-general at the Club House Hotel where he was the licensee. His wife had been doing the job but she had to go to Tasmania for medical reasons. Truth be told, the patrons of the dining room said, while not wanting to be disrespectful to Mrs Davis, Dulcie was the better cook.

The Club Hotel harked back to the days when it was one of thirteen hotels in the town. On the corner of Reid and Myers Streets, it was built in 1879 on the site of Wilcannia's first hotel when the town was buzzing. In those days, the main street was sand and horses were tethered to the verandah posts. When Hazel and her family made the town their home, the place, while it looked grand, was still rough and ready. The population was around 100, with just over half Aboriginal. Hazel felt she was fortunate not to have been brought up racist; her family treated everyone the same despite their skin colour. Apart from anything else, they knew what it was like to have a tough upbringing.

Tregenza wasn't the only 'piss-wreck', as they were known among the more sober townsfolk, but he was one of the better known. Hazel thought of him as being 'well worn'. He had a habit of nodding his head to the left when he said g'day, which Hazel thought showed he still had a spark of cheekiness.

He would come into town from the outlying stations five or six times a year on a bender and liked to stay at the Club Hotel. His practice was to hand Mr Davis his bank book and his cheque book to look after. It meant he couldn't lose them, they wouldn't be stolen while he was in a stupor, and Mr Davis could bank money on his behalf at the Commonwealth Bank — and it also meant Mr Davis always got paid because he held all the cards.

Mrs Davis had felt sorry for Tommy and it had been her custom to offer him bowls of soup and cups of tea, to make sure he had some sustenance between drinks. It was during one such bender in December 1956 when Mr Davis asked Tregenza if he wanted a cup of tea that the fact he had a tidy sum in the bank slipped out. And Dulcie was hovering around in the dining room in the background to hear it.

'I can afford a cup of tea, Stan,' Tregenza replied. 'I've got two thousand pounds in the bank, eh, old mate!'

Dulcie brought him both a cup of tea and a bowl of soup and sat down to talk to her new friend — which was when she learnt he had no family and his favourite soup was pea soup. She dug out a recipe.

Dulcie had hooked Tommy, and she slowly reeled him in. He was no match for her.

The lease came up for the dining room at another of Wilcannia's three hotels, the 1870s Court House Hotel. The single-storey building with its wide verandahs covering the pavements on two sides backed onto the Darling River and was opposite the town's courthouse and police station. For years it was the most popular hotel in town.

The Bodsworths had settled into life in Wilcannia, the first time they had dared put down roots. It was sufficiently isolated and far enough away from Victoria for Dulcie to feel as though she didn't have to look over her shoulder every day for someone from Ted Baron's family to find her.

Harry was working as a caretaker at the local aerodrome and Dulcie took over the lease of the Court House dining room and set about ruling the roost. The family still had their Nash but they didn't have to use it as their bedroom any longer. A galvanised iron cottage behind the hotel came with the job, which was where Dulcie, Harry, Allan, the twins and their half-brother* lived. There were a couple of bedrooms, a bathroom and a tiny kitchen but Dulcie didn't have to worry about the kitchen because she could use the one in the hotel. The walls were whitewashed and it was quite primitive but it was more than they had been used to. The twins and their half-brother enrolled in the local school. The twins looked upon Harry as their father and Harry treated them as his own kids. He had matured fast himself and moved on from when he thought they were a bit of a nuisance. He even enjoyed their company. Allan got a job as a farm labourer.

While they had become well known in town and the surrounding area by then, Dulcie still did not let all her fences down. She never drank nor smoked nor swore, not even a bugger or bloody or shit. It was not appropriate for women to talk like that, she said. Ever the hypocrite, Hazel thought; she had murdered but she wouldn't

---

* Deliberately not named to protect privacy.

swear. Dulcie still hid the real person with all her secrets. Hazel knew that behind her smile and her façade of kindness, she had not changed one bit.

Hazel was still living in the nurses' quarters and was not very happy about her mother being in town instead of kilometres away on a farming station. It was too close for comfort. Dulcie would walk along to the hospital to see her or send one of the kids to tell her to come down to the hotel. Hazel felt that she had little choice in the matter. She found it hard to be disobedient and out of both duty and fear, she would always go and visit Dulcie, never expecting any sign of affection from the woman she had long ceased calling mother. She was never disappointed.

Dulcie's attitude towards her oldest daughter was getting worse as she felt more settled and confident. Nothing Hazel did was any good. Hazel realised the constant belittling was her mother's way of maintaining control but while it was so frequent that it should have been like water off a duck's back, the words could still sting — even though Hazel knew they were not true. What hurt the most was when Dulcie expanded the personal insults to include the rest of Hazel's social group and indeed the whole town of Wilcannia. No one liked Hazel, Dulcie said — no one. She would never amount to anything.

As well as copping the insults, Hazel was still handing over most of her wages to Dulcie every fortnight. Hazel told herself she did it to help her brothers and sister but she knew that it didn't do to get on Dulcie's wrong side.

Hazel wasn't given to huge bursts of excitement, being rather a level-headed young woman and because she hadn't experienced much in her life to get excited about. But she was looking forward to getting married. After they met, Bill had gone back to work on his parents' property at White Cliffs, getting lifts into town when he could. His family had a house in Wilcannia where he stayed and where he had the use of one of his parents' two cars. That 'vacancy' that Dulcie had talked about on Netallie Station had long fallen through when the Bodsworths were chased off the property, but after six months of the long-distance relationship, the ever-thoughtful Bill got a job in town and moved there full time to be close to Hazel.

Hazel hadn't told Bill of her suspicions that Dulcie had murdered her father or that she had somehow caused Sam Overton's death. It all sounded rather far-fetched in the cold light of day and she wasn't ready to burden Bill with all that. She did, however, confide in him about her upbringing and how cruel Dulcie had been. Coming from a big, close and loving family who wouldn't lift a hand against each other, Bill felt very sorry for Hazel and while he couldn't imagine such a childhood, he believed every word. When he knew what to look for behind Dulcie's mask, he could see for himself how hard a woman she was. When he proposed to Hazel, it wasn't with the romance of red roses and getting down on one knee. It was much better than that.

'We should get married and then I can look after you and you won't be scared of her,' he said with insight and meaning every word.

Hazel realised even at the time that she didn't know what love was, not 'love' enough to get married. She'd always thought love would be something that would sprinkle fairy dust on her and pick her up and fly her around the room, like in the *Peter Pan* book. Her feet stayed firmly on the ground and, as she saw, so did Bill's. Neither of them was given to flights of fancy, which was just fine. 'Peas in a pod,' Hazel thought of them as. She did like Bill, liked him a lot, but knew she was marrying him primarily to be safe from Dulcie, and she was so grateful that he had promised to protect her. She felt like fifteen going on fifty with all the secrets on her shoulders and never having had anyone to lean on. She wasn't being cruel but she thought that she could divorce him down the track if things didn't work out.

Knowing all that in her own mind, she was still looking forward to the wedding day and to setting up home with Bill. They decided to get married as soon as they could and the date of the wedding was set for 25 March 1957, the day after Hazel's sixteenth birthday, which was the age of consent back then. Her birthday fell on a Sunday that year so the marriage took place on the Monday.

Dulcie tried as hard as she could to spoil the wedding. She was livid both that Hazel was moving further away from her influence and also that her daughter might just have found the contentment that had always eluded her. Dulcie and Harry put on public displays that they were in love, kissing and holding hands, but Hazel always thought it was more of an infatuation. Dulcie treated Harry like a son and he was dependent on her. It seemed to Hazel that Dulcie always felt there was something better, as evidenced by the way she had discarded her first two husbands.

Then there was the fact she wouldn't be getting any of Hazel's wages any longer, as they would be shared with Bill.

First Dulcie declared she didn't like Bill's family, although she had never met any of them. She made it clear she wouldn't be going to the wedding, which didn't worry Hazel. Dulcie decided they were rich snobs even though she had no idea how well off they really were — Hazel thought it better for Bill's health not to tell Dulcie that he came from money. Then Hazel asked Allan to give her away and he was proud as punch to say yes, but Dulcie belted him, taking a leather belt to his back. Then she banned the rest of

Hazel's brothers and sister from the church service and they were all too scared to oppose her.

So Hazel asked one of her brothers-in-law to give her away but remained apprehensive right up to her wedding day in case her mother came up with something else to try to ruin it at the last minute.

Dulcie didn't even go with her daughter to choose a wedding dress. Bill's mother Elizabeth took on that important role. Bill was a man of few words and he hadn't told his family anything about Hazel's upbringing. Elizabeth just thought that Dulcie was a difficult woman to get along with and wanted nothing to do with the wedding.

Hazel's mother-in-law was a lovely country lady, the sort of mother Hazel would have chosen for herself — warm, open, loving and, most important of all, straightforward. Hazel admired her. She drove Hazel the 200 kilometres down the Barrier Highway to Broken Hill, which was the nearest big town, where she told Hazel to pick out what she wanted. Together they selected a white bridal gown, all billowing white tulle skirt and fitted top. In another break with tradition, the wedding was also paid for by the groom's parents. Dulcie was seething about the whole wedding but she couldn't do anything about it.

Bill and Hazel got married in the Wilcannia Catholic Church after Hazel had sent the priest away with a flea in his ear when he suggested they get married during mass. Those services took ages and she might be a Catholic but she wasn't going to sit in a church for four hours for anyone.

In the beautiful historic sandstone building, Bill's family welcomed Hazel as their newest daughter-in-law. Bill's parents and siblings and Hazel's friends from Wilcannia Hospital were among the eighty guests that filled the small church. She saw Connie

Paterson and her boyfriend Robert Knox sitting in the pews along with other nurses and ladies they worked with including some of the Aboriginal women. Hazel was happier than she had ever been, even as she walked down the aisle with the doubts in her mind about what love was. She also felt a great sadness about not having her father walk beside her and give her away.

However, she didn't miss her mother, not even at the reception, which was at the Country Women's Association hall where Dulcie had a name for putting on a great wedding spread. On this day, everyone brought a plate and Bill's parents put on the beer and wine. All in all, it was one of the most peaceful days of Hazel's life thus far. By the end of the day, she could almost relax because Dulcie had not been able to spoil it.

The newlyweds moved into a little unlined fibro shack on the way out to the aerodrome. Their first home was a bargain even then at 100 pounds. There was no way they would ask Bill's family for any money; this was the start of their own little adventure, their life together, and they needed to do it their way. It was exciting. It had dirt floors and consisted of a lounge room, a bedroom, kitchen and laundry where they had one of those green top-loading washing machines. It was like the ones Dulcie had told Hazel about when she was working as a domestic in the big houses, only second-hand. Not that it mattered.

The couple lined the walls of the shack with newspaper and flour glue. When the paper fell off, they slapped some more glue behind it and stuck it back on the wall. Newspaper was a good insulator. Having lived part of her life in the back of a car, her first real home was like a palace to Hazel and she treated it as such. She covered the dirt floors with lino and paper, which she could shake the dust out of or replace. Hazel put up rods and curtains across the corners of the bedroom to use as wardrobes. Their furniture came from the tip but it was scrubbed with kerosene and then washed down with soap and water. The bed base had no legs so they set it on four drums and bought a good second-hand mattress, pillows, one pair of sheets and a set of pillow cases. There was only one window in the house and Hazel hung up old sheets over the curtain rod as a curtain.

At the tip they found an enamel kerosene stove which had a tank alongside it and they used it for cooking and heating. Hazel scrubbed down a door, also brought back from the tip, which they rested on two drums and which did as a table. She made hand-sewed cushions for another four drums which served as their dining room chairs. After a few months of married life they splashed out on a second-hand red laminex table with four vinyl chairs even though they worried they were being a bit flash.

On the back verandah was a charcoal cooler in which they kept butter. It was a simple timber frame with charcoal-filled sides kept continually moist so the warm air drawn through the charcoal evaporated and thus cooled it down. It was about as basic as you could get and Hazel was amused decades later when the climate-change lobby took up the idea as something they had invented. They used powdered milk and bought meat as they needed it. Hazel was just thrilled when they could afford a second-hand fridge.

It was probably the cleanest fibro shack in the country. Hazel loved keeping it spotless and cleaning everything. Visitors commented how it always smelt of polish. Outside, the small garden was bright with zinnias. The best thing was that she was so happy being with Bill and if that was how love felt, it was something very special. Bill loved taking care of his young bride and they slipped into married life easily. They were like kids playing at being grown-ups and it was fun.

Some evenings when they sat on the back verandah, resting after the meal that Hazel had lovingly made, she could smell the dry red soil as she breathed in deeply through her nose. It was as fragrant as any flowers and for the first time in her life, she felt that her soul was at peace. She was proud of what she had created with Bill. They liked being together in what felt like their little world. If only the outside wouldn't intrude.

One person who never visited their new home was Dulcie. She could look down and see her daughter's married home from the family's cottage further up the hill but Hazel never invited her to come inside and Dulcie was far too proud to ask. However, there were times Hazel could feel her mother's eyes on her even from that far away.

Dulcie hated losing control of her daughter and when Harry told her that a job had come up for a general hand at the aerodrome, she told him to ask Bill if he wanted it. It sounded easier than farm work and Bill accepted. Hazel even wondered — ever so fleetingly as it turned out — if Dulcie had softened because she was being nice to Bill. Some evenings after work at the hospital, Hazel and Bill even had dinner at the Court House Hotel where Dulcie worked. There were no takeaways in those days.

The hotel had a large dining room at the back behind the bar where the guests all sat around a table about the size of a billiard table. Dulcie always had two choices for the evening meal. It started with soup — which was pea soup when Tommy was there — then there was always a meat pie on the menu plus either lamb chops or chicken depending on what the butcher had fresh that day, and a dessert, which was often apple pie with custard or cream. Dulcie's meat pies and apple tarts were legendary.

Dulcie was still a good-looking woman. She preferred the company of men to women and she was still a flirt. Men were, after all, the weaker sex. She had also realised that she could influence men much more easily than she could women, and over the road from the hotel were half a dozen of them, and in uniform to boot.

Every morning she was up baking scones and slices, which she put on paper doilies in a couple of tins and took over the road to the police station just in time for the officers' morning tea. For the cops it was manna from heaven; the police had never known it so good. Few of the officers stayed in the town for long; they were stationed to Wilcannia as part of their mandated stint in the bush. At the time, Constable Max Salisbury, who had moved into one of the police houses with his wife, was one of the least experienced men and he was often on the counter when Dulcie walked in. They always had a chat and sometimes his boss, Sergeant First Class Eric Madden, gave him a shout to invite her around the counter and into the big office they shared. Its walls were painted in a drab magnolia colour and the wooden desks had dark green leather insets on the top where she laid out the scones, hoisted herself up on the corner and turned on the charm.

It was a beneficial relationship for the police — and not only because of the beautiful baking and the generosity of the cook. Working in the hotel, Dulcie heard a lot of gossip and, like police everywhere, the Wilcannia cops wanted to know everything that was going on. She loved to talk and it made her feel important that they were happy to listen. She could still turn on the wit and the cops enjoyed her tales from the hotel.

In December 1957, Dulcie confided in them about her concerns for one of her regulars, Tommy Tregenza. The cops knew him well although he hadn't spent a night in the cells because the locals looked after him when he was the worse for wear and helped him back to bed. A lot of drunken activity among the locals, whether black or white, was just part of life in Wilcannia in those days.

Under Dulcie's spell, Tommy had abandoned the Club Hotel and taken a 'room' at the Court House Hotel. It was nothing more than a shed out the back but it had two beds and shared a bathroom. With a small shake of her head indicating that she could do little about it, Dulcie told the police that she knew Tommy was smoking in bed and she was terrified that he would fall asleep in one of his drunken stupors and set himself on fire. Just like she had done with Sam Overton when she spoke of how he liked a drink, which may have led to his 'gastro' problems, Dulcie was planting the seeds of doubt about Tommy's welfare. She even mentioned her concern for Tommy to other regulars at the hotel, always in a kind and caring way.

Pea soup was on the menu again when Bill and Hazel had dinner at the hotel so they knew Tommy was back in town. Dulcie was serving the bowls as everyone took their seats around the big table but when Hazel sat down and picked up her spoon to start on the soup, Dulcie snatched the bowl away from her.

'You can't sit there, that's Tommy's,' she said loudly.

Hazel hadn't known everyone to have 'their seat' before. Her heart started racing and she wondered for a moment if Dulcie had been slipping something into Tommy's soup, poison or just something to make him sleep more soundly. Later she would feel like a coward for not speaking up as she never knew whether Tommy was being drugged. But she didn't want to believe her mother would kill again so, despite the evidence, Hazel dismissed the thought. It couldn't be.

Tommy took 'his' seat and started on 'his' soup, which appeared to be exactly the same as everyone else's and did not seem to do him any harm. Hazel calmed down. She thought that despite being a piss-wreck, he had lived a good life in his own way. It was written in his wrinkles. Like most alcoholics, he couldn't handle big meals and ate little other than soup. But he always appeared to be contented. He never whinged about his lot, even though he didn't have much. Hazel liked him.

It was obvious that evening that Tommy loved Hazel's mother.

'I wouldn't be alive if it wasn't for Dulcie,' he told everyone at the table. 'She's a good woman, that one,' he said as Dulcie fussed around, asking if he wanted his soup bowl refilled or if he needed more bread.

Tommy stayed in town for the next seven weeks. Although it wasn't strictly part of her duties, Dulcie made sure the sheets on his bed were the best the hotel had when Tommy was sleeping in it. She shook the dust out of his swag for him and hung it over the washing line to air it out.

For those seven weeks he shared his room with Jim, one of the twins. Then thirteen, Jim was a bit of a wild kid, wagging school, but he enjoyed Tommy's company. He knew that if Tommy couldn't do you a good turn, he wouldn't do you a bad turn. The teenager hung on Tommy's tales of life as a shearer, living and working on the land. He quite fancied being a knockabout bloke like that himself. The only bad thing about Tommy was that when he had had a skinful, he snored.

When he was on a bender, Tommy rarely left the hotel; he occasionally ventured out, but only as far as the next drinking hole. This time he moved only between his bed and the bar, never even leaving the hotel at all. Dulcie never strayed far, so every time he emerged from his drunken stupors, she was there to put the kettle on the stove for a cup of tea. After he moved hotels, he started leaving his bank book and cheque book with Dulcie for safekeeping. She always knew how much money he had.

Looking back, Hazel could see her mother's swagger return as 1957 ended with a burning hot summer. She seemed happier than she had been for a while. Not that Hazel could have known what was planned. Dulcie didn't pick up a gun or a knife to signal that she was going to kill someone. She always had an agenda but she was much more underhanded than that.

In the middle of January, Dulcie told young Jim to let Tommy have the room to himself. The hotel had a warehouse and she made Jim a room out of hay bales stacked up and roped off. Two nights later, on Friday, 17 January 1958, Jim woke in the early hours of the morning to the panicked sounds of yelling. He ran down the passageway to the hotel where he saw an orange glow coming from Tommy's bedroom.

Hazel was on the night shift at Wilcannia Hospital when a police car pulled up at the emergency entrance at about 3 am. The cops were always bringing in the black fellas when they got into a drunken fight and hurt each other, but this time Constable Max Salisbury carried the patient in from the back of the car wrapped in a blanket. It was Tommy, covered in horrendous burns and just clinging to life. It was all hands on deck as the nurses could see that his trousers and shirt had been almost burnt away and the exposed parts of his body were red raw after a fire had erupted in his bed at the hotel.

Constable Salisbury told them how Dulcie had knocked on the door of the police house about 2.30 am, waking up him and his wife.

'Come quickly, quickly. Poor old Tommy went to bed smoking and now he is on fire,' she said.

The officer ran to the hotel where he found Tommy still alive, lying on the floor of his room, which was full of steam and smoke. The wall behind the bed was scorched and black but the fire had been put out by Harry.

Dulcie told the officer that she had been woken by the smell of smoke and found Tommy on fire. After grabbing the hose and pouring water on the fire, Harry had picked up a blanket and beaten out the flames that engulfed Tommy's body. She had told Harry and Jim to throw the smouldering mattress in the river to make sure the fire was fully extinguished.

Tommy was put on morphine for his excruciating pain and given fluids to replace those he had lost as part of the body's response to burns. But the hospital wasn't a specialist burns centre and Connie, as a registered nurse, was being realistic when she said she didn't think Tommy would last the night. Hazel couldn't look away from this frail elderly man. He died at 9 am that morning, aged seventy. Dear God, she thought, dear God. What has Dulcie done now?

The town was buzzing with the news of the fire. Everyone was calling it a tragic accident. Old Tommy had fallen asleep in bed drunk with a lighted cigarette and whoosh, he had gone up in flames. Hazel had no evidence that it had happened any differently but it still did not sit right with her.

Just as exciting to the gossips was the news that Tommy had left everything to Dulcie. Well, she had been so good to him and he didn't have any family. Word soon got around how she caught up with Constable Salisbury in the main street at midday the same day Tommy died and handed him an envelope. On the back of it was written 'The last will and contestant of Thomas Tregenza'. Salisbury knew it should have been 'testament' but figured Tommy had misheard the word and didn't know any better. It looked official and Dulcie said Tommy had given it to her but she had never opened it and didn't know what was in it.

Salisbury put it in his pocket and opened it when he got to the station. It contained Tommy's will, signed by him, witnessed by Dulcie and with her named as the executor. In it, he had left her everything he had in the bank, which turned out to be 600 pounds. It was a small fortune, equivalent to around $19,000 today. There would have been more but his bank book showed that on 5 December, 300 pounds had been withdrawn from his account and another 200 pounds had been withdrawn just two days before his death. The money was never found and the police figured it must have been destroyed in the fire.

Unlike Ted Baron, there was enough money to give Tommy a funeral, as basic as it was, and he was buried in the local cemetery among the saltbush and gum trees. Like Ted Baron's grave, there was no one to tend to it and, like Ted, he would have disappeared into obscurity had it not been for what later transpired.

Seven days after Tommy died, the local magistrate opened the inquest into his death, which was never considered suspicious but rules dictated there be a hearing because it had been a sudden death and Tommy had not seen a doctor in so long that there were no medical records. For the second time, Dulcie was called to give evidence at an inquest.

In the witness box of the Wilcannia courtroom, opposite the hotel where she gave the locals the best feed they had ever had and next to the police station where she had charmed the officers with her baking, Dulcie took the oath to tell the truth, the whole truth and nothing but the truth. She told the court that Tommy had been accustomed to smoking in bed and had given them a scare just a week before his death when he fell asleep in an old lounge chair and burnt himself. She said that the night before he died, she had offered him some soup but he declined and went off to bed, holding a bottle of spirits. The next thing she knew she was woken by the smell of burning. As Harry attacked the flames with a hose, she grabbed the smouldering mattress, pulled it to the riverbank and pushed it into the water to make sure the fire was out. Then she ran for Constable Salisbury.

Besotted Harry Bodsworth was as naïve as ever. While other men would probably have started to suspect their wife and worry that they might be the next on her list, Harry blithely sailed through. He was totally bewitched and Dulcie was still coquettish around him both in public and more importantly in the bedroom. It got her the attention she loved.

Harry told the inquest how Tommy's mattress had been in flames and he had quickly picked up the shearer in his arms and laid him gently on the floor. Tommy had been totally in shock. 'I'm all right, Harry. I'm all right,' Harry heard him say.

Constable Salisbury picked up the story from when he arrived at Tommy's room. The late Sam Overton's shooting mate, Dr Potts, as the head of the hospital, gave evidence about Tommy's cause of death. On 29 January, the magistrate, sitting as a coroner, returned a verdict that Tommy had died from the effects of burns accidentally received.

His death knocked the stuffing out of Hazel. She had been on duty when Sam Overton died and now Tommy. Not to mention sleeping metres away from where her father had drowned. She was sixteen, married and working as a nurse's aide and in that part of her life she felt mature beyond her years. On the other hand, she was still only sixteen and right now she felt like a little girl, a scared little girl. The only time she had discussed the family's secrets was with Allan. He was her eyes and ears inside Dulcie's home.

Hazel didn't want to burden Bill with them but as the months went by and summer turned to winter, she needed to share her thoughts and talk through what had happened. The secrets were wearing her down. She felt exhausted.

It must have shown because one evening Bill told her she looked worn out. Hazel took that as her cue. She decided to tell Bill what had happened. There wasn't an easy way to tell your new husband that you thought your mother was a serial killer, but she did wait until after they had eaten dinner. The kerosene lamp cast a dim glow in the room as they sat on the only chairs they had, around the dining room table. She tried to tell him gently but it all came out in a rush. She started with what she thought had really happened to her dad. Until then, Bill knew only that Ted Baron had drowned. Hazel told him about finding her dad's dog 'missing'.

She looked at Bill to see if he somehow disapproved of his new wife's old life. Perhaps he wished he hadn't married into a family of mad people when his family was so stable? She saw that he was looking at the ground. Hazel moved on to her suspicions that her mother had poisoned Sam Overton. She told Bill about how Allan had seen her mother filling capsules with white powder to give to the farmer. She said she believed Dulcie had probably drugged Tommy Tregenza so he wouldn't wake up when she set him on fire.

She got the reaction she had expected from Bill — he couldn't believe her. Not that he thought she was lying but it was all so far outside his own experience that he couldn't fathom those sorts of things happening as she said they had.

Hazel didn't get upset at what he said. She thought her husband was a real optimist: if you don't talk about it, it will go away. It will never happen. Just ride it out and everything will be fine. She wished she could do that herself.

When she told him that Dulcie had poisoned Sam Overton, Bill became animated.

'How do you know that? How can you be sure? You weren't there.'

When she said she thought her mother had killed Tommy Tregenza, Bill questioned whether she was being a bit paranoid. Hazel had once wondered that herself.

Hazel felt that she was behaving like a bitch, always thinking the worst, while Bill was so nice he didn't like to cause any ripples. Contrary to the idiom that a trouble shared is a trouble halved, Hazel didn't feel the burden fly off her after sharing her concerns with Bill, but it had helped a bit to finally talk to someone other than Allan. Unlike Bill, she knew it wasn't going to go away.

A couple of weeks later, Bill came home to their fibro shack from work at the aerodrome bruised and shaken after Harry had knocked him over with the scoop of a bulldozer. He told Hazel that Harry had apologised for the accident. No harm done, he said. Hazel made him sit down and take it easy.

Just a few days after that, she was at work when Bill was brought in to the hospital. This time he had a broken ankle as well as more cuts and bruises. He had been knocked into a hole by the bulldozer driven by Harry. Bill said in what was a whisper only for her ears that he didn't think it was an accident but that this time Harry had meant it. He was even starting to believe in Dulcie's murderous past.

Hazel went cold. She was too numb to take it all in.

A few days later as Bill was at home with his leg up on one of the oil drums they used as stools, Hazel was chilled to the bone again when her brother Allan was brought into the hospital unconscious. Dr Potts examined him but was unable to make a firm diagnosis of the cause. What saved Allan's life was an iron lung, which had been donated to the hospital by a former patient, a wealthy benefactor, because in those days an iron lung cost as much as a house. It was a terrifying contraption to look at. It was an airtight cylinder in which the patient lay with only their head outside as pumps changed the pressure inside to push and pull air in and out of their lungs. Dulcie called in during visiting hours to sit by his side, trying to look like a concerned mother, but Hazel didn't want to go home and leave Allan, especially with Dulcie hanging about. She stayed with him as much as she could while every moment expecting the worst. 'Stay alive, whatever you do, stay alive,' she urged him.

With his head outside the iron lung, Allan could eat and Hazel fed him small amounts by hand. She washed his face for him and brushed his sandy hair. As he got better, Allan was able to talk and after three or four days, he was allowed out of the lung for periods of up to thirty minutes at a time to sit up and move his limbs. In some ways it was a special time for the brother and sister because they had had little chance to be together, just the two of them, since Hazel got married. That was not only because they no longer lived close to each other but also because Allan was still a bit cowed by his mother, who had made it clear that she did not like him spending time with Hazel and Bill. Dulcie had tried to prise them apart, telling Hazel that Allan was 'being difficult', and although she did not go into details — and Hazel knew enough not to ask in order to keep the conversation as short as possible — Hazel sensed that she was being blamed for Allan's behaviour because the two of them were so close.

Prior to his admission to hospital, Allan had been diagnosed with a chest cold and prescribed antibiotics in capsule form. He was still living at home and he told Hazel that he had noticed some of the capsules seemed loose and some were a slightly different colour, as if they had been tampered with. Now they wondered if Dulcie had been tampering with them. They had no reason to think that she would kill her own son, but by now they could be forgiven for feeling paranoid.

As she looked after Allan in hospital, Hazel told him about Bill's accidents at work and it was Allan's blood that froze. He revealed to his sister that a few weeks earlier, he had heard Dulcie tell Harry that Hazel was getting out of control and that she needed to be 'brought into line'. Dulcie had 'suggested' that Bill have an accident at work. Allan was horrified to think that Harry had actually taken her suggestion as an order and carried it out. He hadn't warned Hazel at the time because he thought it had been one of Dulcie's throwaway lines and never suspected that poor weak Harry would act on it. But Harry was deep under his wife's spell.

As Hazel sat by his bed, Allan also told his big sister that he had known before Tommy died that Dulcie was getting everything in his will. She had told him.

'He's not got long to live,' Dulcie had said, but Allan just thought it was because Tommy was drinking himself to death.

However, the two of them did have a laugh — because Dulcie had in the end got nothing. She had taken the will to the bank expecting to be able to withdraw the 600 pounds there and then but the bank manager said he would have to get a solicitor to check it out. She was livid when they told her that it was illegal to be the beneficiary as well as the witness on a will. Then the owner of the Court House Hotel put together Tommy's bill, which ate up a lot of what was left.

When Allan recovered, the doctor still could not diagnosis what had landed him in the iron lung but surmised it had been a consequence of his bad cold. He was sent home and told to rest from work for another week but as a result of their chats, both he and Hazel felt very shaken. She worried that Dulcie was getting 'gamer' but she did not know what to do. Who would believe her? She couldn't report what were, after all, just suspicions. If Dulcie thought she was on to her, goodness knows what would happen.

A couple of days later when Hazel called in at the Court House Hotel to see how her brother was recovering, she witnessed Dulcie and Harry at loggerheads in the kitchen over something. It was unusual to see them arguing because Harry was a total doormat.

'Hazel, if anything happens to me, you tell them that Harry's already done one murder,' Dulcie turned to her daughter and said.

Hazel was gobsmacked. She was at the same time amazed that her mother had finally admitted it to her and emboldened because she thought Dulcie was taking her into her confidence as she used to do. It took her back to 1950 and made her feel like a daughter again.

In that moment, Hazel got cheeky.

'And I know who that was,' she said.

'No, you don't,' said Dulcie.

'Yes, I do. It was Dad — that's who he murdered,' Hazel said, but before she could finish, Dulcie lifted her right hand, hit it across her cheek and knocked her down on the floor.

'How can you say that? You don't know that,' Dulcie said.

Hazel realised that her mother was shocked; she really hadn't thought anyone had worked it out and instead of taking Hazel into her confidence, everything she had said had all been bravado. Hazel quit while she was ahead, let it drop, said goodbye to Allan and fled home to Bill.

Hazel wasn't in the wilderness any longer — she had Bill by her side and that did make her feel safer. It had given her the confidence to confront her mother. But love brought with it responsibility and she didn't only have herself to worry about any longer. Now she began to worry about Bill. Dulcie had got away with three murders and the death of her father's dog. Would there be another one, especially now that she knew Hazel was on to her?

She started to imagine the terror of her dad when he was being held down in the river, groggy from his sleeping tablets. There was the shocking pain she had witnessed Sam Overton go through. She hoped Tommy had been at least partly anaesthetised from all the grog and whatever Dulcie might have slipped him in his soup on the night he died. What would be next?

Hazel couldn't sleep; every noise she heard through the night she thought was her mother come to burn the house down. She knew Dulcie was an arsonist — there were the two properties at Burragan Station as well as Tommy's death. Bill had been injured by Harry. She thought Dulcie was treating them all like playthings and none of the grown-ups could stop her.

Even at work, Hazel couldn't stop shaking. She had been avoiding Dulcie but she was terrified that it was only a matter of time until something even worse happened. She felt like a rabbit, sticking her head up above the ground only to retreat back into the safety of her burrow. Dulcie was getting bolder with each crime she planned, but who would believe Hazel? There was no evidence. Dulcie had the police eating out of her hand; they wouldn't believe anything this bad of her. But she had to be stopped from doing more damage. All those whispered secrets of don't tell your dad, don't tell Harry, Sam and Tommy saying what a good woman Dulcie was, became a roar in Hazel's ears. She couldn't see a way out.

Until it all became too much.

CHAPTER FIVE

HAZEL

THE LIGHT WAS DIM, THE WALLS BARE AND COLOURED PALE green, and the narrow mattress Hazel was lying on was hard. The room she recognised very well — it was the one private room at Wilcannia Hospital. As soon as she opened her eyes, she began to sob. Great heaving cries until she could hardly breathe. Her friend Connie, who was now the matron, pushed through the door and held her hand, telling her to shush and it would be all right. Connie thought that she had never seen anyone so afraid.

When Bill had come home from work the evening before, his eighteen-year-old wife could barely remember looking up at him from her chair on the verandah. He'd asked her what sort of day she had had and she couldn't speak. Instead, she had started to cry. She couldn't stop the tears and then she got the shakes and began vomiting. It was 1959 and he had never seen Hazel in a state like this in the two years they had been married. He took her to hospital; Connie was on duty and thought Hazel had a virus or a bacterial infection, which was why she was put in the private room in case it was contagious. Over the next twenty-four hours after tests showed she had no infection, Hazel had to come to the realisation that she had suffered a breakdown. She was given a mixture of sedatives, but while they made her feel calmer, they couldn't make her feel any safer.

Bill knew people talked in such a small town so he asked Connie to tell the staff not to tell Dulcie what had happened. Connie picked up on the panic and told hospital staff not to let Dulcie visit Hazel. She couldn't tell them why because she still didn't know herself, but she just told them that Hazel needed total rest.

Hazel had never taken more than an aspirin before and the sedatives hit her with a thwack. She slept for three days. As matron, Connie was still in the nurses' quarters next door and as much as she could, she looked after Hazel. In her dazed sleepy state, Hazel started to talk. She started murmuring something about poison on lamb chops and her father's dog still sitting next to the river waiting in vain for him to come back. Connie was very worried about her friend and encouraged her to talk in more detail when she was awake.

The next evening, after Bill had gone home, Connie took her last cup of tea of the day into Hazel's room and found her sitting up in bed leaning back on the pillows and wanting to talk. With her voice still raspy from the drugs, it all came pouring out about her dad, about Sam Overton, her suspicions about Tommy's death. It was the first time Hazel had voiced her fears to anyone outside her family but Connie was her best friend.

It was also the first time she had seen the cool and calm Connie looking flustered. Connie stood up from the hospital chair, looked around the room and sat down again, as if unsure about what she was hearing. Her face was drained. While it should have been the other way around, it was Hazel who put a consoling hand on Connie's arm. She thought she had gone too far.

'I'm sorry, I'm so sorry. I shouldn't have said all that,' she said.

To Connie, it all sounded like a novel set in a foreign world. Yet Hazel was a sensible young woman and she couldn't imagine her lying. Connie had no choice but to accept what she was being told. She knew she had to help and simply asked Hazel what she could do. Hazel said she feared it was all becoming too easy for Dulcie.

She likened it to driving a car. The first time you drive, you are so careful; the second time behind the wheel you are more confident. The third time you feel as though you have been driving for years and it is all too easy. After three murders, Dulcie was on cruise control. She had moved into her comfort zone and she thought she could take whatever she wanted because no one could stop her. No one she knew about anyway.

Connie had seen Overton suffering with gastro and had also been on duty when Tommy was carried into the hospital in agony. It was beyond her comprehension that her friend's mother who cooked them all meals at the pub could have killed them but she could tell that Hazel believed it.

Hazel said that she thought she was the only person who could stop Dulcie before she went any further. Like most people, Connie put her trust totally in the police and suggested that she go down to the station and bring one of the officers up to the hospital where Hazel could talk to him.

Hazel wasn't so sure. She knew the only way to put a halt to Dulcie was to get the police involved but she didn't think the Wilcannia officers would believe her. Number one, she wanted to tell them, but number two, she was too scared. The three of them seemed to like Dulcie. They might even have Hazel declared mental if they thought she was telling such dreadful 'lies' about poor Dulcie. She was also terrified that if they spoke to Dulcie,

Dulcie would come after her to exact revenge. Being family meant nothing to her — she had walked out on four children and got rid of another four. Hazel had no reason to trust her.

Connie had been reducing Hazel's medication and on her fifth day in hospital when Hazel was feeling like herself again, Connie persuaded her that she had no choice but to talk to the police. The two friends came up with a plan to bypass the local cops.

Connie walked down to the police station where she told the officer on the desk that she needed to talk to a detective about something someone had told her. There were no detectives in Wilcannia and, at Connie's insistence, the officer called the much bigger Broken Hill police station where there were forty-eight officers including a detective sergeant and two detective senior constables. As the hospital matron, she was almost town royalty and had a bit of pull.

The Wilcannia officer wasn't able to tell the Broken Hill police much but it was only a couple of hours' drive to find out what the story entailed, so the detective sergeant had one of his senior constables drive him in their unmarked four-door Ford Customline down the Barrier Highway. Having been told how toey the matron was of anyone finding out she was talking to them, they parked around the back of Wilcannia police station. There were two reasons they didn't go straight up to the hospital. One was that they needed to talk to Connie privately. It was early evening, but before they did anything else, the detectives had to make sure she was on the level. The second reason was a matter of courtesy — out-of-town police always introduced themselves to the local boys.

As matron, Connie was used to medical crises that involved dealing with the police so she was calm and deliberate as she passed on what Hazel had said. She said she wouldn't have involved them if she didn't think there was something to Hazel's story. When they asked her if she believed Hazel, Connie was sure. 'I believe her,' she said.

Two detectives lobbing up to the hospital would have got people talking, especially dressed in their 'corporate' outfits. In those days, all detectives — even in the bush — wore a suit, tie and hat. It was as obvious as wearing a full police uniform. They drove Connie to the hospital and left their jackets and hats in the car as she led them through a back entrance.

Hazel felt silly talking about something as serious as this while wearing just a white hospital gown. She also felt at a disadvantage sitting up in bed. Connie stood guard at the door of the private room while the detectives pulled the visitors' chairs up to the side of the bed, where they could sit down instead of standing, which made Hazel feel a bit more at ease. The senior constable got out his notebook and started to make notes as Hazel began with her father and told them all about her murderous mother.

Broken Hill was a wild outback place, the 'Silver City', built on the world's largest discovery of lead, silver and zinc and the reputation of the hard men who mined it and drank their wages. Despite this, there was little violent crime because Broken Hill was a union town and the unions implemented a tough regime. So the two detectives sitting at Hazel's bedside had heard nothing like the story she had told them and they immediately realised it was way out of their league. They had to call in the big guns from Sydney.

Hazel was terrified of what might happen if they left her in Wilcannia once investigations began into Dulcie's past. She told the officers she couldn't go home. Despite the care they had taken, word would soon get around Wilcannia and back to Dulcie that the detectives had been in town and the reason why. As for the detectives, they knew they had to get down on paper what she had told them and get her to sign it off straight away. Connie had sent someone to get Bill to come up to the hospital and he brought some clothes for Hazel. It was after 11.30 pm when the talking stopped and Hazel's life changed forever.

Connie signed her out of hospital and, in the dead of night, Hazel said goodbye to Bill. She would always remember that as Bill hugged her at the back door of the hospital, some red-tailed black cockatoos lifted out of one of the gum trees. She felt as spooked as they did. She got into the back of the police car and made herself as comfortable as possible on the sticky vinyl seats. Then she was smuggled like contraband out of town and away from Dulcie.

At Broken Hill, while it was only early in the morning, the detectives knocked on the door of one of the motels and woke up the owner, who seemed to Hazel to have been woken many times before by the cops. The senior constable stayed with her while his boss went back to the police station and called the CIB in Sydney. He was told to make sure they took a typewritten statement from Hazel, got her to sign it and put her on the first plane down to Sydney. All police know the adage that there is a trip in every job, so the two Broken Hill cops felt they both had to accompany their witness on the flight. It would give them a couple of nights' drinking in the city with their Sydney colleagues, who had to show them the courtesy of joining them. The first flight back to Wilcannia wasn't for two days. Sweet as a nut, as they said.

Commercial flights to Sydney from Broken Hill left three times a week, arriving before lunch and leaving just after. There was one that very day. Never having flown before, Hazel was given a window seat on the Fokker Friendship. As the earth fell away, she realised she had escaped but had no idea what awaited her. It was all happening so fast. Strangely, she wasn't scared about the future. It was either that or retreating to the shadows for the rest of her life. She felt like a weight had been lifted off her shoulders because she had been able to pass some of the responsibility for what to do about Dulcie onto others. It was like walking up to a window with the dark behind her and opening the curtains to let in the light.

Dobbing in her mother wasn't easy but Hazel told herself it had to be done. She put aside the few fond gestures there had been between mother and daughter and pretended that Dulcie was no relation, just a woman who had committed three murders. And one of the things she would have to confront was how everyone thought Dulcie was so nice. Hazel knew that she had to stay strong to survive.

Detective Sergeant Raymond William Kelly was waiting for her on the tarmac at Sydney Airport. The first thing she noticed were his hands — they were huge. The whole of Ray Kelly was very imposing. He was as tall as her father had been, over six feet, and he was a snappy dresser wearing a light suit with a white handkerchief pointing out of the top left-hand pocket, a white shirt with a tie with wide stripes and the obligatory hat. In his case it was a fedora. His face was a bit aristocratic if craggy and he wore glasses which were partly rimless with a black slash across the top. Hazel thought he looked dashing. She didn't know his history or his reputation but she immediately felt that with him, she was in a safe pair of hands.

Kelly had been accused of many things since fulfilling his childhood dream of joining the police in 1929 but subtlety was not among them. He was once seen hanging a suspect over the balcony of Sydney's CIB headquarters by the ankles as he shouted: 'Confess or I'll drop you.' As a young cop barely out of probation, he had chased a stolen car — on his bicycle. When the driver found himself in a dead end and reversed, knocking Kelly off his bike, Kelly made his first headline arrest. He leapt onto the running board of the car, grabbed the steering wheel and drove into a shop window. Then he took two of the criminals from the car into custody but only after shooting them and killing their mate, the driver, with a shot to the head. He got his first of eight commendations for bravery.

Born the son of a brewer in Wellington, New South Wales, Kelly cut his teeth in the mines of Broken Hill and as a jackaroo in Queensland before joining the police where his toughness and charisma became the stuff of legend, nurtured by the headlines in Sydney's tabloid newspapers whose reporters and photographers just happened to turn up when Kelly made a major arrest. He knew the power of the media and Sydney was his city.

His nicknames spoke volumes about the man — he was known as Gunner, because he shot first and asked questions later, or Verbal, because all of his suspects confessed. At the time Hazel met him he was the most infamous officer in New South Wales if not the whole of Australia — a star detective. It would later be said that he was corrupt but he was a bloody good cop. The sort you wanted on your side, not against you.

One of his many sayings was: 'If a man hits you, hit back. Hard. If a man shoots, shoot back.' In an era when bank robberies and safe cracking were the glamour criminal professions, Kelly had been the head of the safe-breaking squad. He arrested notorious bank robber Darcy Dugan four times, the first time putting him behind bars for shooting a bank manager, the following three times leading the hunts that recaptured him after his celebrated escapes from jail.

Like all good detectives of the day, he was only as good as his network of snitches and Kelly had an enviable network of informants, including crims happy to dob on their competitors. He was as much at ease mixing with the underworld hoods as he was with politicians, celebrities and racketeers, and counted the vice queens Tilly Devine and Kate Leigh among his friends. Kelly had formed part of the bodyguard for Queen Elizabeth II on her 1954 tour of Australia.

Hazel never felt the slightest bit intimidated by this 63-year-old tough-as-nails career cop. When he met her at the airport, he was on his way to being promoted to inspector after leading the manhunt for escapees Kevin 'Simmo' Simmonds and Leslie Newcombe who had escaped from Long Bay jail. On the run, they beat to death a warder at Emu Plains Prison Farm and stole his gun. Newcombe was arrested two weeks later but it took another three weeks, a Navy helicopter, patrol cars, German shepherd tracker dogs, 500 armed police and Ray Kelly to corner Simmo in the bush near Kurri Kurri in the Hunter region where he surrendered and was later jailed for life.

Kelly and his offsider, Sergeant John Palmer, known as Jack, saw a slender, poised young woman walk down the stairs from the aircraft, and Hazel and Kelly hit it off immediately. He couldn't abide whingers and admired Hazel's courage. To him, she was a detective's dream. She was like a tape recorder when she started talking as she remembered amazing details. After bottling it all up inside her for years, Hazel wasn't at all tired of telling the story again. She felt the ghosts of three dead people looking over her shoulder. Not for a moment did she feel guilty about dobbing in Dulcie, whom she had long ago stopped thinking of as her mother.

The officers booked Hazel into a motel under a false name for the first couple of days and to tell the truth, Hazel thought it quite exciting. Kelly and Palmer spent a long time interviewing her and getting it all down on paper with the help of their state-of-the-art Olympia typewriter. Hazel told them there was no way she could go back to Wilcannia. It had hurt her to walk away from Allan and the twins with no explanation but she couldn't risk them knowing what she was doing and where she was. It was safer for them as well as for her. Bill had told them all, including Dulcie, that Hazel had had a breakdown and the doctors had told her to get away from everything. Hazel thought that if Dulcie got even a whiff of the truth, her own death would quickly follow.

Ray Kelly was already one step ahead of her. He introduced Hazel to the twilight world of what he called witness protection. In those days it was a bit ad hoc, not the well-oiled machine it is now with entire police departments devoted to keeping vulnerable witnesses safe, but to Hazel it was no less secretive. Hazel had to walk away from her old life at least until they could secure her safety. Kelly told her she couldn't go home or talk to anyone from home, not even Connie. She didn't have to change her name but she was told not to mention her real surname. Her new home wasn't a fortress, but that is what the anonymous-looking federation house in the suburb of Bexley might as well have been when she was dropped off by Kelly and Palmer.

Not that she wasn't made to feel at home. The elderly couple who were paid by the police to let her live with them could not have been more welcoming. She had her own bedroom with a big wooden wardrobe and a chest of drawers that she knew was called a lowboy, as opposed to a tallboy. After living under the bright skies of a bush town, it took her a while to get used to the darkness of the house with its small windows and the smell of mothballs.

The couple was very polite, sometimes to the point of being annoying, Hazel thought. They were devout Plymouth Brethren and lived a simple, frugal life. The house was always cold and they were careful with the power, turning off the lights when they left a room. The meals were plain and filling, usually meat and two veg. Never three veg. The woman was squat, wore dark clothes and her hair in a grey bun. Her husband looked a bit like her — but without the bun. They never knew her surname and never asked. When Ray Kelly rang, as he often did to update Hazel on his investigation and check on her welfare, he simply asked for her by her Christian name. It wasn't the first time the couple had been involved in this cloak and dagger witness protection, Hazel thought.

The man who would help put Dulcie away for murder knew it wouldn't be easy. The case wasn't straightforward; Hazel had no direct evidence — so far it was all hearsay and circumstantial — but all police know that a circumstantial case can sometimes be more persuasive before a jury than a witness, a body and a confession. Kelly was at the starting gate but building up to a gallop.

He had a lot of work to do and he began tracking down the people whose names Hazel had given him to line them up for interviews. He was going to have to get copies of the inquest findings into the deaths of Tregenza and Overton and may have to get orders for all three bodies to be exhumed. The crucial forty-eight hours after the discovery of any body had long ago expired and he told Hazel that she had to be patient. She had waited this long.

Meanwhile, murderers are no respecters of police time and resources and Kelly had a dozen other cases to solve.

But Hazel was missing Bill and her siblings. She had never lived so far away from her family, either in physical distance or mentally. It was quite liberating, but while she was brave on the outside, there were times when she was still feeling conflicted about dobbing in Dulcie. Hazel suffered bouts of depression, sometimes unable to stop crying as she walked down the street. Her days were long, lonely and scary.

One day she went to see a doctor, a middle-aged man who asked her what was wrong. Hazel blurted out her problems, told him she was frightened of her mother and scared she would find her.

'Your mother killed your father? Do the police know?' the doctor asked from his side of the desk.

Hazel said that the police did know and when the doctor followed up asking whether her mother was in jail, Hazel said she wasn't.

'So you tell me that your mother killed your father and the police know and she's not in jail?' The doctor stood up and walked around the desk.

'I don't believe you. I think you are delusional and I could have you committed for such serious accusations. I could send you to Callan Park.'

Callan Park was a notorious mental asylum left over from the last century. Hazel fled the doctor's rooms. Just as it was getting easier for her to talk about the truth, and just as she thought people were believing her, the doctor's reaction knocked the wind out of her sails.

Bill had never gone back to work at the aerodrome after he broke his ankle. Apart from the police, he was the only person who knew where Hazel was and he missed her as much as she missed him. They hadn't been able to write to each other because while he was scared someone would read the address after he posted a letter, she was afraid someone would see the postmark on letters from her. He had been able to call her from a public telephone box but she couldn't ring him because their home didn't have a phone.

After a month of this loneliness, Bill packed up what he could carry and got a friend to give him a lift to Broken Hill where he caught the train to Sydney. As the train swayed from side to side for over fourteen hours across the flat dry plains, he had plenty of time to think about what the future would be for him and his young wife. It certainly wouldn't be dull. He had put their Wilcannia house on the market and left all their furniture behind, figuring it would end up on the rubbish tip where it had come from. The house sold for 300 pounds and they tripled their investment. For the next nine months he lived in the Bexley house with Hazel who he now looked upon with fresh eyes as being the most courageous person he had ever met.

Kelly thought it would be safe for Hazel to move further afield than Bexley and have a look around Sydney and the couple rented a flat. Dulcie had so far steered clear of big cities and they figured she wasn't likely to be walking around Sydney. Hazel was relieved but she couldn't help looking over her shoulder wherever she went. She was scared that Dulcie would smell a rat and come looking for her.

Until then, the biggest shop Hazel had seen was Knox and Downs in Wilcannia. In Sydney, she was in awe of upmarket Grace Brothers, David Jones, Mark Foy's and Farmers Exclusive Furniture, although she had no money to buy anything. She never complained about having no money just as she didn't like it when people who had money bragged about it. Bill quickly got a job as an offsider on a furniture delivery van with Farmers. Once he knew his way around the city, he graduated to a driver. Having worked as a nurse's aide at Wilcannia, Hazel decided to use her time in Sydney to qualify as a nurse, which at the time was done on the job and not at university. So the couple settled into their new little life.

In Wilcannia, Tommy Tregenza's death was the catalyst for more changes. The six years Dulcie had been in town was the most settled time she had ever had in her life but, like always, she was never contented. She was bitter that she had ended up with almost nothing from Tommy's will, even blaming poor old Tommy for it. She had a fight with the owner of the Court House Hotel over something that years later no one could recall but Dulcie blamed the owner for starting it. She stopped paying him rent for the family's cottage after she lost her job and they were kicked out of their home.

Dulcie and Harry, the twins and their little half-brother moved into a cottage at the aerodrome where Harry still worked. Dulcie found that she could still be important around town with her wedding teas and party catering. The work brought in some extra money but, just as importantly, it meant she was still shown some respect. No one could bake like Dulcie.

Without his sister to rely on, Allan left home. Bill had confided in him where the couple was living and he joined them in Sydney for Easter. He later had an accident in Broken Hill when a horse rolled on him and he ended up working as a station hand on Kangaroo Island, about as far away as he could get from Dulcie.

That gypsy urge to move on again had crept up on Dulcie along with the fact that the family hadn't been able to pay all their bills. She owed money all over town. Although everyone knew her, Dulcie never developed the skills to form deep relationships that led to friendship. She only ever had fleeting acquaintances. One night, Dulcie and Harry packed up the old trailer behind the Nash and sneaked out of town for good with Margaret and her half-brother. They did an old-fashioned midnight flit.

Jim had got a lift back into town after a week working on Duntroon Station way outside Wilcannia to find the house empty and the car gone. Dulcie hadn't even waited to say goodbye. He was fourteen. One of the locals pulled up his ute alongside Jim as the youngster was walking along the main street and asked him what was up. 'Mum's gone,' was all Jim could say. One of the guesthouses put him up for the night for free and the next day he began his working life as a roustabout in the shearing sheds.

In Sydney, Hazel took a deep breath. She was homesick for the bush, homesick for Wilcannia, even homesick for the red earth and the snakes and the muddy Darling River. She broached the possibility of returning home with Ray Kelly and she wouldn't have gone if he had said it was too dangerous. But he figured that with Dulcie having left town under a cloud, she wouldn't dare go back. If she did, Hazel was to go straight to the police.

After almost a year in the wilderness of Sydney, the timing was perfect for Bill and Hazel to return. One of Bill's brothers had bought a spread up in Queensland where he wanted to run cattle and he needed to sell the café he had been running in Wilcannia. The couple moved in with Bill's mum in the family's house in town — with its six bedrooms and six sleepouts to accommodate the whole family when needed — for a month before taking over the Cosy Corner Café with its attached furnished house.

They had been away for almost a year and everyone in town was very welcoming on their return. Hazel felt guilty because she had missed Connie's wedding and she looked with longing at the little fibro cottage she and Bill had once made their own. A white fella and a black girl had bought it and were keeping it nice.

Hazel had inherited Dulcie's baking skills and she was up by 4 am every day baking pies and sausage rolls, which were great sellers. The café was a local institution which had been advertising 'A Long Cool Refreshing Drink … Confectionary and Fruit … Fresh Fruits in Season … served at Keen Prices with Prompt Courteous Service' in the local paper for decades and was a bit of a general store. It was beside the art deco-style Plaza Cinema and stayed open until 11 pm on Wednesday and Saturday nights when they did big business, especially when John Wayne movies were showing. The café was so busy that Bill and Hazel had a local woman helping them, Shirley. She was what Hazel called a rough diamond with a million vices of which swearing and smoking were two.

Jim had fallen in love with one of Bill's sisters, Alma, who sometimes helped out in the café.

Hazel relaxed so much being safely away from Dulcie that she became pregnant and their daughter was born at Wilcannia Hospital in 1960. Sadly, three miscarriages followed, all of them boys, over the next three years. There was no IVF in those days but the doctors told Hazel that her hormones were out of balance and she began hormone treatment.

She would never forget the story Dulcie had told her about dumping three of the children from her first marriage — three of Hazel's half-siblings — at orphanages to grow up without a mum and dad. Hazel had done it tough herself and she knew how lonely and scared you can be when your life is in turmoil. When she learnt that some of the church homes closed for Christmas and needed the children cared for, she and Bill put their names down. The first two children they fostered were sisters Wendy and Betty, aged ten and twelve. They came to Wilcannia from a Presbyterian home in Sydney for the six weeks over Christmas, and Hazel and Bill made sure it was a loving and special time for the sisters.

Still desperate for another child of their own, they spoke to the welfare officer in Broken Hill who had arranged the foster care of Wendy and Betty and he approved them to adopt. He told them not to get their hopes up because it would probably be a couple of years before a child became available.

Hazel was torn between two lives. One was that of a mother and wife seemingly without a care in the world. The other was that of a person living on tenterhooks for the call from Inspector

Kelly to say that Dulcie had been arrested. Sometimes she felt she was barely keeping her balance. While things appeared to settle down, Hazel was still scared that Dulcie would discover that she had been found out, as she put it to Bill. She was lucky that she didn't crack under the pressure.

The Cosy Corner Café had the luxury of its own telephone line so Ray Kelly was able to keep in touch. When Hazel asked the inspector why the investigation was taking so long, he explained that there could be no mistakes. They would have only one chance to get it right.

CHAPTER SIX

MR AND MRS PILL

THE BREAKTHROUGH IN THE POLICE INVESTIGATION CAME IN Adelaide on a morning at the tail end of spring in 1964.

A police team under Detective Inspector Ray Kelly had been meticulously retracing Dulcie's steps going back to even before Ted Baron's body was pulled out of the Murray River. In Wilcannia alone they interviewed sixty-one people, including Sam Overton's in-laws from Netallie Station, the McClures, as well as Madge Fitzgerald and her daughter Lin from Burragan Station. They had spoken to Allan Baron, who was working as a shearer on Kangaroo Island where he had invited his brother Jim to join him.

Bob Wighton was a young detective senior constable at Broken Hill in October 1964 when he was told to meet Kelly at the airport and drive him to Wilcannia. The CIB golden boy's legend had — as always — preceded Kelly, but all the same, Wighton was surprised by his appearance. Wighton was six feet four inches and even though Kelly was a few inches shorter than him at six feet, he made Wighton feel small. The first thing Wighton noticed was

Kelly's huge hands, then his solid, imposing eighty-kilogram frame kept trim by surfing, and the way he walked down the steps from the aircraft with a swagger.

He was huge in stature as well as by nature and Wighton was in awe of this man who was totally in control.

Among police, war stories grew like Chinese whispers and by then, word had got around the Broken Hill and Wilcannia police departments that Dulcie Bodsworth had killed five men. According to the murmurings, she had brazenly pushed her late husband into the Murray River in his wheelchair; she had blasted someone's arm off with a shotgun; and when she left Wilcannia aerodrome, she had poisoned the garden around the cottage and nothing would ever grow again in that patch of land.

Kelly put Wighton right as they drove in the Ford Falcon to Wilcannia. It was three deaths they were investigating, and that was enough.

Kelly's reason for the trip to Wilcannia was to get the lie of the land. He wanted to see where Tommy Tregenza had been killed. Incredibly, out the back of the Court House Hotel, the charred mattress, which had been retrieved from the Darling River where Dulcie said she had thrown it to extinguish the flames, was still there. Wilcannia was the sort of place where an old mattress could lie undisturbed. Kelly knelt down to smell it.

'Geez, mate, get a smell of that,' he said. He reckoned the mattress still reeked of kerosene, which had been poured on it by Dulcie before she put the match to it and set Tregenza on fire. Forensic examination was not what it is now and Kelly didn't have the mattress sealed up to take back to Sydney. Instead he ripped out a sample and put it in an evidence bag.

Most of the physical evidence against Dulcie, however, lay underground, buried in cemeteries across New South Wales and

South Australia. A few weeks after Kelly's visit to Wilcannia, the police made their move.

First thing on 26 November 1964 at Adelaide's largest cemetery, Centennial Park, Albert Hermann 'Bert' Brinkworth joined the New South Wales government medical officer Dr John Laing, Detective Sergeant John Palmer and another Sydney detective from Kelly's team as they walked to plot number 262A in the Catholic section A just off the main roadway. That Thursday morning at 5.30 am, Brinkworth, the cemetery superintendent, led them to the grave where Sam Overton had been resting since his interment on 21 April 1956. It had been over eight years but the gentleman farmer was going to have to be disturbed. They would make it as quick and as dignified as possible.

Armed with a warrant to exhume the body, pathologist Dr Laing carried with him twenty-three specimen jars, which had been sterilised two days earlier and stored in a locked safe at the Adelaide City Coroner's office. Everything was done by the book because they wanted to leave nothing for the defence to challenge in court about the evidence they feared they would find.

The first jar was filled with soil taken from 200 feet away from the grave — a test sample. More soil samples went into the jars at various depths beneath the headstone as the grave was dug up, until the wooden casket was exposed at its depth of six feet nine inches. Every step was photographed, every move logged. The nails holding the nameplate bearing the inscription 'Samuel Overton aged 44 years' next to a simple wooden cross on top of the casket containing the coffin were removed. More soil samples were taken from around the casket and placed in the specimen jars.

Before the morning could get much hotter, the coffin inside the casket was raised from the ground. As the ropes around it hauled it up, gallons of brownish fluid poured from the right corner at the head of the coffin. The bodily fluids filled a four gallon container and some of it was collected in three specimen jars. More soil samples were taken from the moist ground beneath the coffin. The coffin was lifted onto the back of a ute and taken to the Adelaide City Mortuary with a police escort.

By 8.45 am, Sam Overton's coffin was lying on a metal table in the morgue. Inside the coffin was a sealed zinc lining and Dr Laing prised the top off. He wasn't surprised to find the body was still 'well preserved' because the protection of the zinc had delayed the process of decay. To others it would be a macabre sight; to Dr Laing it was another day at the office. Unlike the bodies of Baron and Tregenza, there had never been a postmortem carried out on Sam Overton because his death was put down to natural causes.

His body was dressed in blue and white striped pyjamas and there was still brown hair on the head and a moustache on the upper lip. The pathologist took samples from them, sealing them in more specimen jars. The nails on the hands and the feet were still intact and specimens of them were taken along with some teeth, muscle from his right thigh and portions of bones. Samples were also cut out of the pyjamas.

Significantly, Dr Laing found no evidence of any injury to Overton's body, nor any signs of illness such as a ruptured gastric ulcer that could have caused his death.

When the postmortem was finished, all the specimen jars and envelopes containing other evidence like the clipping from the pyjamas were sealed with sealing wax and placed in two wooden boxes, which were nailed shut to protect the chain of evidence. The boxes were taken to Sydney where it was up to the forensic examiners to uncover their secrets.

Brinkworth, a religious man who had studied at Bible college, had taken it upon himself to clean up the grubby metal nameplate from the casket as a mark of respect to Overton but it was never reattached. It was retained as evidence they had opened the correct coffin. Overton's body was placed in a new coffin with a new nameplate and re-buried that same day.

The police didn't need the permission of Overton's family to exhume the body but they worked closely with his widow Margaret who gave them her backing because she wanted to know the truth. If only Hazel had known all those years earlier that Mrs Overton shared the suspicions that her husband had not died of gastroenteritis but had been poisoned.

'But I never wanted to believe it,' she told journalists who spoke to her after news of the exhumation became public.

In Sydney, detectives personally delivered the wooden box containing the specimens to the government analysts where chemist John Newhaus examined them with remarkable results.

In the liver, kidneys, small intestine and stomach he found traces of arsenic. In the thigh muscle, the nails, the upper part of Overton's right tibia and his teeth — arsenic. In the wood from the casket, in the pyjamas, in the liquid that had leaked from the coffin there was more arsenic. The report to Dr Laing confirmed what they had feared — altogether there was more than enough arsenic to kill one man. In fact, there was enough to kill a few people.

If Dulcie was going to be charged, it was with all three murders and Inspector Kelly had to decide whether to exhume the bodies of Ted Baron and Tommy Tregenza. Their deaths had been for more obvious reasons than that of Overton's and postmortems and inquests had been held to determine the cause and manner of death, albeit it without the extra information the police had now. It was decided not to exhume Tregenza's body but when Kelly spoke to Hazel, she was happy for her father's body to be exhumed.

The fresh postmortem on Ted Baron's body uncovered no more clues to add to what they already knew — he had been alive when he went into the water as the government medical officer Dr Morris had concluded at the time. Baron's air passages were full of fluid. All the witnesses who had given evidence at Baron's inquest were re-interviewed.

It was time to find out what Dulcie and Harry had to say for themselves.

The detectives had been working out of the old CIB headquarters above the police station in Central Lane behind where Sydney's Central Local Court still stands. When the time came to plan the arrests, they had moved into what became known as 'The Old Hat Factory' on the corner of Smith and Campbell Streets, Surry Hills — so named because of the detectives' head attire. Kelly liked to play things close to his chest but it had become time to show his hand.

He had put out an all-states message looking for Dulcie Bodsworth, described as a 'middle-aged woman', and for her husband who was described as having a 'smiling face'. Police across Australia were told they had a son and a dog and that they used a number of aliases including the surname Pill.

In the general duties room, the journalists gathered as they did every morning, smoking, joking, jostling in their competitive camaraderie that lasted only until one of them got an exclusive and all bets were off. That Tuesday morning, 1 December 1964, news had started to filter out of Adelaide about the exhumation of a body. The reporters all knew something big was up and were waiting for their briefing. An astute player of the media, Kelly knew he couldn't keep the breaking news quiet for much longer so he decided to tell them all, off the record with no quotes to be attributed to him. It was the best way to make sure the police controlled what got out and Kelly knew how just a few facts could easily fill a 500-word story and make headlines.

'Now, boys, here's the story …' he began as he always did.

Within hours it was all over the front pages of the papers. 'MURDER. WOMAN HUNTED; GRAVE OPENED.' '3 DEAD MEN. CIB REOPEN CASES.' 'HUNT FOR WOMAN; THREE KILLED.'

At the Cosy Corner Café, Hazel was enjoying being pregnant again. Amazingly, not long after she and Bill were told they had been approved to adopt a baby, she discovered she was pregnant with their second child thanks to the hormone treatment. The day before he told the reporters, Kelly had called the café to let Hazel know the police were going public and that it was only a matter of time before they arrested her mother. She had been waiting for this moment for years and she knew it would come but she hadn't realised how it would feel. It was like being hit by a ton of bricks. She was talking nineteen to the dozen until Shirley got a word in.

'Shut up and have a smoke' was Shirley's solution to everything. The dangers of smoking and pregnancy were not public knowledge in those days.

The café sold cigarettes and Shirley took down a packet of Ascot smokes, which came in fat packs of forty-five. They were nowhere as smooth as portrayed by the beautiful girl who smoked them on a yacht in the advertisement at the cinema. Hazel spluttered and choked but kept at it and didn't stop smoking for another forty years. She did think that Dulcie, who abhorred smoking, would have been horrified. Bill wasn't very happy either.

Over the next three days, the hunt for Dulcie took on a life of its own. The Sydney papers didn't make it to Wilcannia until the afternoon and although she had set all this in motion, Hazel found it difficult to read about it in black and white. In the café,

Shirley tried to deflect attention from Hazel when the locals came in to buy the papers because by then, people had figured out that the police were looking for Hazel's mother, the woman who had at one time or another cooked most of them a meal at the Court House Hotel.

'Drowned, burned, poisoned. THREE MEN MURDERED! WOMAN HUNTED; GRAVE OPENED,' one paper screamed. 'Police are on the trail of a woman who is believed to have murdered three men. Money is believed to have been the motive for all three murders which occurred in remote districts of NSW over an eight-year-period between 1950 and 1958.'

The Sun in Sydney said: 'Sydney CIB has asked detectives in Victoria and South Australia to help them in a search for a woman who disappeared from Wilcannia about six years ago.'

The Daily Telegraph countered with: 'CIB detectives investigating the mystery deaths of two men at Wilcannia and another man at Mildura are expected to make fresh moves early next week.'

The Daily Mirror, *The Sun*'s competition as another Sydney afternoon paper, headlined: 'Triple murder. HUNT FOR WOMAN. Three fatal friendships. Police are seeking a middle-aged woman they believe can help them in their inquiries into the deaths of three men. She worked as a domestic in the country districts where the men died.'

'Exhumation of the body of a man last week followed 15 months of secret inquiries into the deaths of three NSW men,' yet another newspaper article said. 'Police investigations, which started 12 years after the death of the first man, are now believed to indicate that the deaths are linked. At the time the three men died and were buried there was no suspicion that death was not due to natural causes.'

Overnight, Dulcie Bodsworth became the most wanted woman in the country. She appeared to be the only person oblivious to the fact the police were after her.

Dulcie and Harry had drifted back to his home town of Hopetoun in Victoria where Harry still had some family although his milkman father had died four years earlier of peritonitis. Dulcie was working as a cleaner again but was starting to earn a reputation around town as a cook to hire for parties and other events. Harry worked as a labourer on the railways. Dulcie and Harry's son was fourteen and at school. Margaret, at nineteen, had left home but still lived in Hopetoun. Jim had heard nothing from them since they had sneaked out of Wilcannia leaving him behind. Dulcie had never tried to get back in touch with either Hazel or her brothers. It was as if they didn't exist.

After being so open about her real identity at Wilcannia, Dulcie had reverted to her secret self in Hopetoun. Once they had crossed the border from New South Wales, she and Harry stopped to cut up all their old identification papers, including their driver's licences.

Dulcie had once more erected walls that blocked out her past, as she had done with her first marriage and with her first four children. She wasn't hiding from the police, because she thought they would never come after her. It was the last thing on her mind. She had almost wiped the deaths of Overton and Tregenza from her mind. And as for Harry, well, he had helped to kill Ted Baron and tried to get rid of Bill but he had no idea what his wife was really capable of even after thirteen years of marriage. The family reinvented themselves again, taking on the surname of Harry's mother, Pill. The 'Pill' family lived in a rented weatherboard cottage in Dennys Street, one of the rural town's older addresses. They became regulars at a local Baptist church where they both taught about the Bible at Sunday School without a hint of irony.

Happy-go-lucky as ever, Harry was glad to be home and to see his brothers and sisters again, although what he told them about the reasons for taking their mother's name is not known.

The Swinging Sixties hadn't quite reached Hopetoun. No one could have missed the fact that the biggest band in the world, the Beatles, had toured Australia earlier that year but Dulcie had no idea that it was one of Sam Overton's relatives, the dashing war ace, Kym Bonython, who had welcomed them to Adelaide. Despite her racy past, Dulcie remained conservative with a small 'c'. She was fifty-five in an era before fifty was the new thirty and even though it was summer, she still liked to dress properly in a hat and gloves. She could no longer play the ingénue but if she read the newspapers at all, she would have hated the 'middle-aged' tag they put on her. She refused to let herself go and dress like a frump. After all, her husband was still nineteen years her junior and she had to keep up appearances.

That Thursday afternoon, 3 December, she was by herself shopping for groceries as she walked along Hopetoun's main thoroughfare, Lascelles Street, when two police officers in uniform stopped her and asked if she was Mrs Pill. They said they would like her to accompany them to the police station, which she did with a smile. She didn't think they were going to ask her to bake some scones but she was still hoping this was not about what she thought it was.

Before the arrest, Hopetoun police had been in touch with Sydney. Ray Kelly was already on a plane to Melbourne and Senior Detective Angus Ritchie, an experienced homicide investigator from Melbourne, had that morning driven the four and a half hours up the highway.

In Wilcannia, Hazel had received the phone call from Kelly she both welcomed and dreaded.

'We've got her, Hazel. Sit tight. I'll let you know what happens from here,' he said.

Hazel had to indeed sit down. The sun was still shining, there were people in the café, everything looked normal, but Hazel felt as if all the air had been sucked out of her world. Her head felt as though it was full of cotton wool.

She was going to go to tell Bill when the phone rang again with another call that would change her and Bill's lives just as profoundly. Amazingly, there was a baby boy waiting for them at Sydney's Crown Street Women's Hospital. Later, she always said that the news about the baby protected her sanity.

It was a good two days' drive to Sydney and another two days back on a dirt road from Broken Hill as far as Cobar. Bill's parents would look after the couple's four-year-old daughter, and Shirley, puffing away on her Ascots, said she could take control of the café. Hazel and Bill got ready to leave, deciding to drive straight through. There were few motels at that time for travellers and although they could have spent the night in a hotel, they wanted to get there and back as soon as they could. They felt safe in their home at Wilcannia.

At 3 pm in Hopetoun, Dulcie was led into an interview room at the police station and told that Harry had also been brought in. He was in another room for the time being. For the first time in her life, Dulcie Bodsworth was almost lost for words. She knew this meant they were in serious trouble but she still had no idea that her oldest daughter was behind it.

She was given a glimmer of hope when Detective Ritchie handed her a provisional warrant issued out of Sydney for her arrest — not for murder but for arson. She was charged with burning down the homestead and the woolshed at Burragan belonging to that miserable old Madge Fitzgerald and her pathetic daughter Lin.

That liverish mother and sad daughter had always had it in for her even though Dulcie knew they had no evidence. She had even convinced herself that she had never done it. They had just accused her out of spite.

Dulcie was taken before a Justice of the Peace under her real name, Bodsworth, and remanded to the Court of Petty Sessions, as the Magistrates Court was then called, in Melbourne the next day. Harry wasn't charged and he agreed to accompany his wife to Melbourne. At 8.30 that evening, they got into the back seat of the police Ford Falcon with Ritchie in the front passenger seat and a colleague of his driving. Although they had only been separated for a short time, Dulcie and Harry had had no chance to talk. There was always an officer within earshot.

Ray Kelly and John Palmer were driving up from Melbourne and met up with them at Ararat Police Station. It was 10.45 pm and Dulcie and Harry had had no rest. It was of course all carefully staged by Kelly. He could have waited for them in Melbourne and allowed them to have a night's sleep. But he wanted them kept on edge. Ararat was chosen simply because it was around halfway between Hopetoun and Melbourne. Kelly didn't know that one of Dulcie's grandmothers had once been locked up and died in the town's hellish psychiatric hospital, known as the Ararat Lunatic Asylum, which had housed the mentally ill for 140 years.

Even without the insight provided by Hazel into her mother and stepfather, Kelly would have known immediately that Harry was the weak link. He was just so meek and so willing to help. If he hadn't known that Harry had helped drown Ted Baron, Kelly would have thought he was just a down-to-earth hardworking country bloke. As for Dulcie, the officer could see no family resemblance between her and Hazel. They were like the proverbial chalk and cheese in looks as well as behaviour. She was trying to be 'ladylike' but he thought she was as hard as nails.

Kelly liked nothing better than the thrill of the chase and that included getting his suspects to talk. He was known for being ruthless but he was charming and manipulative at the same time — like any good detective. He once said that when he became a detective, he realised that he had to understand people. He read Freud and picked up tips from watching psychiatrists giving evidence in court: 'In this job you must know how much to use a person — and when to stop. I became a student of psychology.'

There was going to be no rest for Dulcie and Harry. Kelly and Palmer spent until 4.15 am talking to them in separate, bare interview rooms during which the couple was left in no doubt that their situation was dire. In records of the interviews, Harry denied killing Ted Baron and Dulcie denied murdering Baron, Overton and Tregenza. There was no food, just cups of tea. At 4.30 am, they were put in separate cars and driven to Melbourne. The Bodsworths were exhausted. Kelly, Palmer and Ritchie were just getting into their stride.

It had been decided that Ritchie should stick with Harry because they had already started building a rapport. It had been Ritchie who arranged for Harry's mother Louisa, who lived in Geelong, to pick up Harry and Dulcie's son in Hopetoun and look after him. While the officers continued to call Dulcie 'Mrs Bodsworth', Ritchie was calling Harry by his first name. In turn, Harry called him Mr Ritchie.

At Melbourne, Dulcie got a shocking dose of reality when at 7 am she was booked into the City Watch House in Russell Street. The stone cells with their heavy black metal doors hadn't changed since the watch house was built in 1909 and Dulcie was searched and locked up in a holding cell on the women's side. At 10 am she was led into court where she faced the arson charges and was remanded in custody to be extradited to Sydney because the crimes had occurred in New South Wales.

Then she had to face Kelly and Palmer again as they had another go at her with an interview that was recorded by Palmer on the typewriter.

'Are you quite prepared to give us all the information that you can regarding Mr Overton's death?' Kelly asked.

'Yes,' Dulcie replied, doing her little-girl-lost act.

'Did it surprise you when Mr Overton suddenly took ill?'

'Yes, it surprised us all.'

'Have you ever been in the "skin shed" or the "killing pen" at Netallie Station?'

'No, I have not.'

'According to your son Allan, he overheard a conversation between you and Bodsworth at Netallie Station in which you said to Bodsworth "If Sam goes you will be all right here always". Did you say that?'

'No.'

'Is it true that you were anxious to remove Overton from Netallie Station in order that your husband could get the position of manager?'

'No, it is not.

'On another occasion your son Allan declares that you requested him that whilst he was on a shooting expedition with Dr Potts and Sam Overton and your husband to accidentally shoot Overton while he was on the other side of the swamp and make it look like an accident. What do you say about that?'

'I say never.'

'According to your son Allan he told you not to be silly when you made such a statement. Do you remember that?'

'No.'

'Your son Allan informs us that on another occasion you said to him "I have always got my revenge on people who have done things to me". Did you say that?'

'No, I did not.'

As Kelly questioned her about throwing boiling water on the poor old cook, pointing a shotgun at Jim and Lance McClure and telling the McClures that Sam had been drinking a lot before his death, it was sinking in to Dulcie that the police had not only done their homework but that Allan and possibly even Hazel were behind her arrest.

When Kelly asked her about Hazel, Allan and Jim, Dulcie began to plant the seeds of doubt about what they had said.

'I want you to tell us whether you ever had any violent quarrels with your daughter Hazel or your sons?'

'The only arguments I have had with Hazel was because I would not say she was older than she was so that she could go to work.'

'What about the boys?'

'No, not really, but when they asked me for things I would not give them they would go crook on me.'

'Do you believe that any one of those three children of yours would wilfully lie to do you an injury?'

'Well, after what I have seen from you I could not say anything else but yes.'

Meanwhile, Harry was taken by the nice 'Mr Ritchie' over the road to the Homicide Squad offices in the Russell Street Police Station where he was offered breakfast.

'Thanks, Mr Ritchie. I do feel hungry. We never had time for tea last night,' Harry said politely.

At the Homicide Squad offices, he asked to use the phone to speak to the minister of the church the couple had been attending in Hopetoun. As he hung up, he broke down and cried.

'You don't know how I have worried about this for years. I knew you would catch up with us sooner or later and I am glad now,' he told Ritchie.

Harry said they had used the surname Pill because they didn't want Hazel to know where they were, even though it meant them missing out on child endowment payments all those years. The truth was that they had changed their name to hide not from Hazel but from Wilcannia after their midnight flit. They owed so many people money.

Ritchie asked him: 'Did you tell Mr Kelly the truth last night?'

Harry said that the statement he had made about Ted Baron at Mildura was not correct and he did 'know something about the death'.

Ritchie cautioned him that he did not need to say anything unless he wanted because anything he did say may be given in evidence in court. He bought Harry breakfast in the cafeteria at the police headquarters and then Harry asked if he could talk to his wife alone after she had appeared in court.

It hadn't taken long to break Harry Bodsworth. There were so many moving parts in this investigation and Kelly had decided to throw a few more into the mix. It was now time for Harry to learn some harsh home truths about Dulcie's past.

After all, a crime leaves no room for secrets.

CHAPTER SEVEN

RAY KELLY

'YOU DIDN'T TELL ME ANYTHING ABOUT CAVANAGH!'

Harry stood with his back against the grubby wall of the interview room while Dulcie sat at the stained table, still with her hat on. The room stank of the thousands of cigarettes smoked in there; it also smelt of despair.

Dulcie didn't look up.

'No,' she said.

'You didn't tell me that the girl Ruby was your daughter, did you?' he said.

Dulcie's head shot up. She realised the police had been doing their homework and now it seemed her husband knew her secrets. Taken totally by surprise, she could see no way to lie about it.

'No,' she said.

'You didn't tell me anything about getting three hundred pounds and two hundred pounds from Tommy Tregenza either, did you?' Harry said, according to police notes of the conversation.

'No, I didn't get three hundred pounds from Tommy, I only got two hundred pounds,' Dulcie said defiantly. As if the other one hundred pounds would have made any difference.

'You didn't tell me you got the two hundred pounds off Tommy Tregenza either did you?'

'No.'

'This man here told me that you paid one hundred pounds to Knox and Downs store a few days before Tommy Tregenza died. You didn't tell me about that either, did you?'

'No.'

Dulcie began to cry. When Hazel heard much later about the tears, she thought it was another remarkable performance from her mother. As far as she was aware, Dulcie never cried. She shed no tears when she dumped her four children, nor when she lost the other four to miscarriages. She could tell hard-luck stories until the cows came home but it was all for sympathy. Dulcie wasn't the sort of person to feel sorry for herself. She had killed three men including her own husband without shedding a tear. She possessed no conscience. She was lethal.

Hazel figured that like the stories, the tears were put on for pity. As an act, it didn't work on the cops who just watched on patiently, but it worked on Harry even as he realised she had hidden half her life from him. He would still walk over hot coals for her.

Dulcie's faithful husband of thirteen years put his hands on the back of her chair. He really did love and care for her.

'How much more haven't you told me?' he said.

Dulcie kept silent.

'Why don't you tell the truth about everything? You would feel much better if you told the truth. I have told the truth now and I feel better already. If you had anything to do with the deaths of

Tommy and Sam, why don't you tell this man about it? Did you give Sam arsenic?'

'Yes, I gave it to him on a chop for breakfast.' Detectives Kelly, Palmer and Ritchie had been watching the confrontation but even they were surprised by her sudden admission. At this point, Kelly gave Dulcie the same warning that Harry had received. She did not have to answer questions unless she wanted as anything she said may be used in evidence. Dulcie sobbed that she understood.

The police had choreographed it to perfection.

It had begun that morning after Dulcie got back from court and Harry asked if he could talk to her alone. They had both denied anything to do with the deaths of Baron, Overton and Tregenza. Since police suspected both of them were involved in murdering Ted Baron, normally the detectives would keep the suspects apart but this wasn't a normal case. Leaving the couple together in an interview room was a gamble they thought would work. It did. After about ten minutes behind the closed door, Harry walked out. 'All right, Mr Ritchie, I am now prepared to tell you what happened at Mildura.'

Detective Ritchie went into the room with Harry and asked him if he had discussed this with his wife.

Dulcie's performance reached new heights. Quick as a flash she said: 'Believe me, it is a shock to me but I intend to stick to Harry. Baron was no good. He was very cruel to me, Mr Ritchie.'

Harry was led away by the nice Mr Ritchie to make what was his second statement while Dulcie was left to stew for a bit longer. She had still only been charged with the two counts of arson.

Ray Kelly moved into the picture to conduct the interview with Harry. This was it. After five years of investigation, they were getting to the truth. Kelly turned down the swagger because Harry Bodsworth wasn't a crim whose face Kelly had to get into. He could sit back and play the nice guy because he just knew that Harry was the kind of person who would feel obliged to answer the questions. The veteran detective appeared relaxed but, like his colleagues, his mind was working hours ahead. Harry didn't know how tough Kelly could get when he needed to.

Kelly realised as soon as Harry began to talk that the couple had decided he would take the blame for Ted Baron's death. Kelly let him say what he wanted. Harry couldn't explain how the crippled Baron got onto the beach beside their tents but said that Baron had started an argument with him which turned into a struggle.

'He called me a few mongrel bastards, Mr Kelly,' Harry said. 'And I said shut up, you rat, and I gave him a push and he fell back into the water.'

He said Baron floated out and was carried away in the fast-flowing muddy water and disappeared.

'Dulcie knew nothing about it, Mr Kelly. It was an accident,' Harry said.

His story was full of holes but it was as good a confession as any and Harry was charged with murder. Wasting no time, that evening, Kelly and Palmer accompanied by a senior Melbourne detective flew Harry to Mildura. At 6 am he led them down a trail from the main road to the beach on the banks of the Murray River and Harry pointed out where Baron had gone into the water. Times had changed so much in the past fourteen years that the only families camping along the river that December were those who liked a life on the road, or holidaymakers. Social security benefits meant people didn't have to live rough unless they chose to.

It was a different world but as the sun began its ascent, Harry could recall exactly where he had camped in 1950 with Dulcie and the kids. He pointed out the tent site and walked the police through the struggle he had had on the beach with Baron before the little group drove back to the airport and flew back to Melbourne.

Back at Russell Street headquarters, it did not appear that the seriousness of the charge had sunk in for Harry — perhaps because of the metal plate in his head. He thought that in light of his statement to police and how open he had been with showing them what had happened at Mildura, the matter would be closed. When he was asked if he wanted to see a solicitor, he told the police: 'No, I have given it a bit of thought and I will wait to see what happens.'

Detective Ritchie had to explain to him in simple terms that Dulcie would be extradited to Sydney and he would be sent to Melbourne's Pentridge Prison while the Victorian police carried out a full investigation including re-interviewing all witnesses because the Murray River was on their patch. Harry wanted to know how long he would be kept locked up and was told that would be up to the courts.

Harry became very quiet.

'Will you be talking to my wife about this?'

Told that Dulcie would be interviewed again, Harry said: 'Well, I might as well tell you the whole truth. It is no good doing things by half; you will only find out in the long run.'

Ritchie made a note that Harry had 'some moments of thoughtful pause' before speaking again to tell Ritchie that when he and Dulcie had been allowed to talk privately the previous morning, they had decided that Harry would take the full blame for Baron's death so she could look after their young son 'but it doesn't look as though that is going to happen'.

The truth, said Harry this time, was that Dulcie had asked him to kill her husband. She had planned it three weeks before Baron had got back from the hospital so that she and Harry could get married with her husband out of the way. They had waited until Baron was snoring with his sleeping tablets: 'I picked him up when he was asleep and carried him out to deep water and let him go. He just sank.'

In his own handwriting, Harry wrote out his third and final version of what took place at Mildura on 30 and 31 August 1950.

Hazel had been right about her suspicions even though she had been just nine years old. Not that she knew about Harry's confessions. At the same time Harry and Dulcie's world was falling around them, Hazel and Bill were on their way to Sydney to meet their newest family member even as they kept another secret close to them.

Harry was hot and tired and Detective Ritchie arranged for him to have a shower and shave. As he towelled himself dry, he asked Ritchie how come the police knew so much about what had happened all those years ago. It was then that Ritchie told him that they had been talking to Hazel and her brother Allan. After consulting with Detective Kelly, Ritchie took Harry into the Homicide Squad's general duties room where he was shown the statements from the siblings, which had been removed from the rest of the file. Ritchie told Harry more about the details of Dulcie's first husband, Ted Cavanagh, and their children.

It was all part of the choreography staged by the police. Harry was left spinning. He was shocked at first, then angry. He asked to talk to his wife again. As he and Ritchie joined Kelly and Palmer, who were talking to Dulcie in the interview room, Ritchie looked up at the clock and noted it was 6.45 pm. The officers later told a court that they didn't know what was going to happen when they let Harry talk to Dulcie — but they had left nothing to chance.

They watched in silence, with Ritchie taking notes.

After Dulcie admitted to putting arsenic on Sam Overton's

breakfast chop, she said she didn't know why she had done it. There was no mention of how she coveted the big house or measured up Overton's clothes and boots for Harry.

'Why did you poison Overton?' Harry asked.

'It is terrible, I don't know why I did it,' she said. 'He never did anything to me. It is a terrible thing I did.'

Dulcie said she had got the arsenic from the skin shed: 'Sam told me to go to the skin shed and he told me to get a cup of arsenic and he told me how to mix it to poison the weeds and the ants around the garden.'

'I always thought you might have had something to do with Tommy but I didn't think you did anything to Sam. If you did anything to Tommy Tregenza tell this man about it because it doesn't matter how many more you have done,' Harry said, appearing deadly calm.

When Dulcie did not answer, Kelly prompted her: 'Did you have anything to do with the death of Tommy Tregenza?'

'I did, I burnt him. I put a match on his bed,' Dulcie admitted.

Kelly said: 'Bed clothes would not ignite in a way they did in this room unless there was some inflammable substance present. Did you place anything or pour anything in the bed?'

Dulcie said she regularly used methylated spirits on her legs because it was supposedly good for aching muscles and she was usually on her feet all day cooking. The night Tommy died, she took the bottle from her bedroom and poured some of it on his bed before setting a match to it. She said he had gone to bed drunk and she didn't think he would wake up.

'It was really going when I got into the room. I thought there must have been something [an accelerant] there,' Harry added.

Dulcie said she was too upset to do a formal interview that night and was taken back to the cells.

*

Ray Kelly was used to crimes that propelled him into the headlines but even he had never arrested a multiple murderer before. The term serial killer was not coined until over a decade later by FBI veteran Robert K Ressler, the real-life Jack Crawford from *The Silence of the Lambs* and the man upon whom Agent Mulder from the TV series *The X-Files* was based. As a supervisory special agent with the FBI's elite Behavioral Science Unit, Ressler devised the science of 'criminal profiling' but despite the advances in predicting the behaviour of violent criminals, he always said that profiles didn't catch killers — cops on the beat did.

Kelly knew that it was usually only with hindsight that murderers looked evil. If they looked like killers they would not have been able to lure their victims and ply their trade. Most murders are driven by greed, by sex, by hatred, by revenge, in panic, in a rage. Dulcie Bodsworth was the most unlikely serial killer. Middle-aged, mundane and appearing respectable, she killed because she wanted something and three men had got in her way. She did not even hate any of her victims. She never saw what she had done as wrong and even managed to justify her actions. Kelly wondered if she was a psychopath.

Ressler had interviewed over 100 murderers in prison including most of the world's notorious serial killers. But they were all men. The highly respected Ressler said that serial killers are mostly male, white and in their twenties or thirties at the time of the murders and the exceptions were so rare that he had never interviewed a female serial killer. He wrote that his extensive research had only come up with one female who was arrested and accused as a serial killer — Aileen Wuornos. Wuornos became known as America's first female serial killer after she robbed and shot dead seven men in Florida between 1989 and 1990, claiming they had raped or tried to rape her while she worked as a prostitute. She was executed by lethal injection in 2002 aged forty-six.

Dulcie Bodsworth had entered an exclusive and wicked group. Around the time of her arrest, on the other side of the world in England, the so-called Moors murderers, Myra Hindley and Ian Brady, killed five children between July 1963 and October 1965. Four of their young victims were sexually assaulted and at least three buried on Saddleworth Moor, hence the name given to their killers. They were arrested not long after the death penalty was abolished in 1965 and jailed for life.

In the 1980s, the deranged Perth couple David and Catherine Birnie lured five women to their suburban home in Moorhouse Street, Willagee. They chained and handcuffed them, tortured and raped them, murdering four of them before the fifth, Kate Moir, somehow escaped through a window on 10 November 1986 and ran for help. She had left evidence she had been in the house by hiding pictures she had drawn and remembered the name she saw on a medicine bottle — David Birnie. They were also jailed for life.

There are few female serial killers in Australia who acted alone. Babysitter killer Helen Patricia Moore was one of them. In 1979 and 1980, Moore killed three of the boys and girls she was babysitting at Claymore and Dharruk in Sydney's west, including her fourteen-month-old stepbrother and a cousin, aged sixteen months, by smothering them to death. Her last victim was her brother Peter, seven, who she said had fallen down the stairs. She had strangled him to death and her own mother took her to the police station and made her hand herself in.

Another female serial killer was Kathleen Folbigg who was convicted in 2003 of murdering her three infant children and of the manslaughter of a fourth between 1991 and 1999. Their deaths had been put down to natural causes until her private diary, discovered by her husband when the family had moved to Singleton north of Sydney, revealed otherwise. The prosecution case was that Kathleen couldn't cope with the demands of motherhood and had smothered the children. Aged forty-nine at the time of writing, she is serving a thirty-year jail sentence with a non-parole period of twenty-five years.

*

On the morning of 6 December 1964, one of the first of Australia's female serial killers had regained her composure and some of her control. She had had a good night's rest despite the noise from the other cells.

Ray Kelly and Angus Ritchie sat down opposite her in the interview room, with Kelly doing the talking and Ritchie the writing this time. A non-smoker like Dulcie, Kelly hated the stench in the bleak interview room as much as she did but they were stuck in there all day as he took her through the three murders. Ressler noted that most serial killers like to boast about what they had done. Not Dulcie. She was casting about for one of her famous escape plans, a plan B, but there wasn't much to go on.

Dulcie said that drowning Ted Baron had never been discussed. She said she had been helping Tommy Tregenza who was old and infirm and setting fire to his bed had been a spur of the moment thing.

Then Kelly moved on to the death of Sam Overton, the murder that the police had most of the evidence on against Dulcie. This time her answers were closer to the truth.

'How long had you been using the arsenic for poisoning the

ants and the weeds before you started to give it to Mr Overton?' Kelly asked.

'I would say a fortnight.'

Kelly: 'Will you tell us on how many occasions and in what manner you administered the poison to Mr Overton?'

'Once on his own and once when he had a meal with us. I sprinkled it over the vegetables and the chop and I poured gravy over the chop. I know I put a good bit on.'

Kelly: 'Did Mr Overton make any comment about the taste of the food after he had eaten the food with the arsenic on it?'

'Yes, only the once. He said it tastes bitter, but he kept on eating.'

Kelly: 'How long after the first dose of arsenic did he become ill?'

'I am not quite sure. It could have been that night or the next day.'

Kelly: 'When did you give him the second dose?'

'If you ask Harry, the day after Mr Overton had his dinner with Mr Daniel English, he might be able to tell you. That was the day I gave him the second dose in the morning with his breakfast. He didn't have vegetables then, he had chops and eggs. I think I put gravy over the chops.'

She had given the second dose within a week of the first one, putting on a 'fair bit. I put my fingers in a couple of times and sprinkled it over his food.'

Kelly: 'Did Mr Overton complain to you about his condition after you had given him the poison?'

'Yes. He said he had the stomach ache, he had diarrhoea. At one time he said "A man would be better off dead".'

Kelly: 'Who got the doctor to come and see Mr Overton?'

'I did. When he got very sick I got worried. I rang the doctor a couple of times and he said to bring him into Wilcannia but he wouldn't go. Then when he got real sick we rang the doctor on the quiet and I think I went off and got the doctor … I should have told you the truth from the start.'

Kelly: 'Your son Allan has informed us that on one occasion when Mr Overton was going out shooting with Dr Potts, your husband and the parish priest, you told him to shoot Sam Overton and make it look like an accident. Is that correct?'

'I am up against it there. I don't know whether I told him that or not.'

When it came to reading through that final record of interview, Dulcie admitted she couldn't read very well and another police officer was brought in to read it all through to her before she signed every page.

The next morning, Kelly and Palmer sat next to Dulcie and Harry Bodsworth in the back row of the economy section and were flown to Sydney after their extradition from Melbourne. Neither of them had been on a plane before but this was no time to enjoy the thrill. Dulcie was livid with Harry for buckling but continued to be nice to him to keep him on side.

Kelly had decided not to handcuff them but made sure the media were tipped off to get the shots of the couple arriving to face justice. Dulcie and Harry had been taken from the airport to the 'Old Hat Factory' where the charge against Harry for murdering Ted Baron in the state of Victoria was withdrawn and he was freshly charged with 'feloniously and maliciously' murdering Baron in the River Murray near Buronga in New South Wales.

At 3.35 pm that day, Dulcie was finally charged with the 'felonious and malicious' murders of Ted Baron, Sam Overton and Tommy Tregenza.

The couple who had not been apart for one night since their marriage in December 1951 were split up. They were taken by separate prison vans to Long Bay jail where Dulcie was placed in what was then known as the Women's Reformatory at the State Penitentiary Centre. She had to swap her coat and hat for prison attire. Harry was locked up next door in the men's jail and they would only see each other again in a courtroom dock.

The photographs of Dulcie and Harry made it onto the front pages of that afternoon's newspapers. Hazel had to confront these shots as she and Bill drove along Crown Street in Sydney on their way home to Wilcannia with their adopted son. It was the first time in five years that mother and daughter had been in the same city or town and even as she tried to feel brave as she held the baby boy to her chest above her six-months-pregnant belly, Hazel was totally unnerved.

She couldn't stop sweating and shivering and felt ill all the way back to Wilcannia. That night when they stopped the car to get some sleep, Hazel couldn't rest. She was feeling unwell when they got home and then realised she was bleeding. A miscarriage at six months is unusual and at the hospital, the doctor could give Hazel no answer as to why she had lost the baby so late in the term. She and Bill were devastated.

He was a new doctor and didn't know Hazel's past and she didn't tell him that the woman all over the news who had been charged with three murders was her mother. He didn't make the connection as their names were different. But Hazel knew why she had lost her baby. She put it down to the stress and panic of realising that she was going to have to face her mother in the not too distant future and stand up to her in public.

She was in turmoil.

CHAPTER EIGHT

DEL FRICKER

'MRS BARON, HAVE YOU EVER TOLD A LIE? YES OR NO.'

In the witness box, Hazel took her time answering public defender Fred Vizzard QC's first question. He was so short and old she thought he looked like a Chihuahua with a smirk on his face that was as mean as all get out. This was the fourth time she had given evidence and this was the sort of trick question she had come to expect from him. She had grown to dislike this fancy lawyer who liked to play ping pong with questions and answers. It made her feel that she was the one on trial.

She thought if she said no, the jury would know she was lying because no one had never told a fib. But if she said yes, Vizzard would make it a big deal. She thought about saying she had told little white lies but Vizzard told her the answer had to be yes or no. So she told the truth and said yes.

Vizzard turned to the jury in the seats on his left so his black robe wafted around him like the dark smoke that accompanied the appearances of the Wicked Witch of the West in *The Wizard of Oz*. He waved his arms in true theatrical barrister mode: 'This woman admits to being a liar.'

That afternoon it was all over the front page of *The Daily Mirror*: 'Daughter admits to being a liar.' Next to it was a photo — of the wrong woman. It wasn't Hazel. It was a woman totally unconnected to the case although strangely she had the same surname. It was the only thing Hazel could laugh at, given the prospect of having to face her mother six times in the courtroom — three times to give evidence at committal proceedings to determine if there was enough evidence to send Dulcie to trial, and then three more times during the trials.

The prosecution decided to proceed in order of the deaths with the first committal for the murder of Ted Baron beginning on 16 February 1965 in the imposing wood-lined Central Local Court on Sydney's Liverpool Street. The first time she saw her mother after all those years, Hazel fainted. She was in the public area waiting to give evidence on day one when there was a scuffle. She looked up to see Dulcie in handcuffs being led into the court by Ray Kelly and another officer, with Dulcie trying to get to Hazel.

She heard Dulcie say 'Oh Hazel, oh Hazel' before Hazel hit the floor as if she had been shot.

Later that day, Dulcie asked if she could talk to her daughter. It was highly irregular for a defendant to speak to a witness — never mind a key prosecution witness like Hazel — but the police thought something valuable might come out of it. They stayed in the interview room as Hazel was led in to meet with her mother. All Hazel could recall afterwards was Dulcie looking down and seeing cigarettes in her handbag.

'Oh my God, they are not yours, are they? Hazel, I hope you don't smoke,' Dulcie said.

Hazel lied that the cigarettes belonged to Bill. Such was the strange dynamic that existed between mother and daughter. Hazel was prepared to give evidence saying her mother was a murderer but afraid to own up to smoking. Despite all that had gone on between them, Dulcie could automatically revert to being the one in charge.

Seeing her unease, Ray Kelly gave Hazel a guardian angel to guide her through the marathon court process. Sergeant Adele Dorothea Fricker, known as Del, would later be dubbed the 'powder puff detective' but this trailblazer for women was anything but a 'powder puff'. Like Hazel, she knew that women could be tougher than men, emotionally if not physically. In the days when female officers were given police-issue handbags but not handcuffs, and just three years after policy was changed to allow women who married to remain in the police force, Fricker was a favourite of Kelly's. Less than a year later, Del Fricker would show her mettle when she acted as bait to lure notorious armed robber and murderer Ronald Ryan to his capture after he escaped from Melbourne's Pentridge jail.

Ryan was a career criminal serving an eight-year sentence for a series of breaking and entering offences when on 19 December 1965, he and fellow prisoner Peter John Walker made their escape at 2 pm as the guards took turns to attend the staff Christmas party. They stole a guard's M1 carbine rifle, which Ryan used to shoot dead warder George Hodson as the prison officer pursued them. They grabbed a prison chaplain as a human shield before rifle-butting him in the head.

As a national manhunt got under way, the desperate fugitives fled to Sydney where Walker sought to catch up with a former girlfriend, a nurse at the Concord Repatriation Hospital in Sydney's west. She wasn't at home when they visited her house but her daughter was — and she recognised Ryan from the blanket media coverage of the escape. There was also the suggestion that one of Ray Kelly's legendary network of informants, the powerful career criminal Lennie McPherson, had betrayed Ryan when he and Walker had asked for help to get false passports and cash to flee the country. In an elaborate sting, the nurse agreed to meet Ryan and Walker, saying she would bring along a friend for a double date. They arranged to meet at 9 pm at the gates outside Concord Hospital in Sydney's west, the fugitives unaware that the couples, hospital staff and passers-by were really plain clothes police officers.

In all, fifty armed marksmen led by Kelly had staked out the area.

Fricker was called on to work late after her day shift to act as the 'secret date'. Her job was to protect the nurse at all costs, even to take a bullet for her if necessary. 'Get in front of her and see she runs to safety,' were Fricker's orders.

On the warm summer evening, the women waited in the dark for half an hour and had just walked into the hospital for more instructions when Ryan and Walker turned up. They were quickly arrested by Kelly, shotgun in hand. On 3 February 1967, Ryan became the last person to be hanged in Australia when he went to the gallows at Pentridge jail.

Del Fricker had joined the police in 1951, the year after Dulcie and Harry killed Ted Baron. A former kindergarten teacher, she went on to receive a Commissioner's Commendation for her role in the capture of Ryan. Her work later earned her a British Empire Medal and the Queen's Police Medal for bravery.

In 1967 she joined the CIB Drug Squad and in 1971 she became one of the state's first two female detectives and Del's 'D' girls were born. She ran the twelve-strong elite female detective section, which was likened to *Charlie's Angels*. The TV series was then at its zenith and breathless newspaper reporters wrote: 'To the hardened crims of Sydney's underworld, they are Del's "D" girls.' 'Like TV's Charlie's Angels, they fight crime with feminine flair and fervour.' 'They can handle a gun or a tight situation with the same ease as a lipstick or mascara brush.'

In an interview many years later, Fricker, ever pragmatic, said she never had a problem with the way those first female officers were portrayed. 'You have to remember the seventies brought worldwide change when we had women like Germaine Greer telling us to burn our bras,' she said. 'It was doing our job and doing our job well that mattered and the men never excluded us. We were a team.'

Fricker also appreciated the fact that the police were one of the only employers at the time that paid women the same as men.

She and Hazel hit it off straight away. Hazel knew she needed someone to rely on and her trust in Del Fricker was not misplaced. Del quickly became Hazel's rock. She guided her through what was going to happen and told her about court etiquette, but most importantly she kept Hazel calm and boosted her confidence, giving her the courage to keep getting into that witness box.

Bill and Hazel's two kids were too young to understand what was happening and far too young to be told. How would their parents tell them that their grandmother was a murderer who had killed their grandfather? Hazel and Bill told them that 'Mum and Dad have to go and do something important' and left them with Bill's family when they were flown to Sydney where they were put up in a motel. In plain clothes, Del Fricker accompanied Hazel to court every day.

At the committal hearing, the prosecution was represented by a police prosecutor, Sergeant C Bush, who was organised and disciplined but lacked the flair and practised sarcasm of a trial lawyer like Fred Vizzard. The prosecutor began by calling witnesses who had given evidence at Baron's inquest including Captain Bill Collins who had found the pyjama-clad body in the

Murray River, and William Corby, then a sergeant, who had been the constable who investigated Ted's death. Ray Kelly and Angus Ritchie were called to give evidence about the confessions made by the two defendants. But the star witness was Hazel.

Both Fricker and Kelly had warned Hazel about Vizzard, the state's well-known sole Public Defender who was paid by Legal Aid to defend Harry and Dulcie. Outside of the courtroom he was said to be rather shy, but he hid his shyness with tenacious advocacy inside the court. He was actually very good at his job, it was just that Hazel did not like to be on the receiving end of his modus operandi.

Vizzard had a practice of sitting in the waiting room outside court reading *The Sydney Morning Herald*, then a broadsheet. To try to put witnesses off balance, he read the paper upside down. Hazel had been warned he would try to intimidate her but she knew he could never be as intimidating as her mother.

As she walked through the swinging doors and along the right-hand side of the court to the witness box, Hazel was aware — without having to look — of her mother sitting in the big dock to her left, next to Harry. Dulcie still scares the shit out of me, she thought. Del Fricker and Ray Kelly were sitting in the public benches, which were full. After she swore the oath to tell the truth and took her seat, Hazel looked up to see both Dulcie's and Harry's eyes on her. Dulcie wore a green knitted three-piece suit that Hazel had never seen before and she carried a light green veiled hat on her lap. Harry wore a dark blue suit; it was the first time Hazel had seen him dressed up since his wedding.

The defendants weren't the only ones in their Sunday best. Hazel had dressed carefully, terrified she might not make the right impression among the important people who would be at court. She wore her favourite double string of pearls, one cream, one black, and a white sun hat which she took off before going into the courtroom.

Feeling very alone in the witness box, Hazel told the court how Dulcie and Harry met at Wangaratta in the camping area, about their affair while her father was still alive and the Aspros and hot milk her mother gave the kids to sleep the night he was killed. She got to the bit where her father's dog Toby howled on the riverbank after her father died 'as if he was calling for him and that gave us the idea that Dad …'.

Vizzard leapt to his feet and objected to the relevance of the evidence about Toby. 'Going to call the dog?' he asked sarcastically.

Sergeant Bush countered that he would show how it was relevant. He asked Hazel if anything was said by Dulcie or Harry after her father died.

'Yes. One day Mum said it is a good thing dogs can't talk and Harry said yes,' she said.

At those words, Hazel heard a murmur around the courtroom and she realised that the men sitting at the large wooden table to her right were reporters, excitedly scribbling in their notebooks. 'Dog to be prosecution witness?'

'Did you hear your mother tell any police officer anything about the man Bodsworth?' the prosecutor asked.

Hazel: 'She said he was her brother. That is all I heard.'

Prosecutor: 'Did you ever hear your mother speak to other people in the camping area or at Mildura about her relationship with Harry Bodsworth during the time they were in Mildura?'

Hazel: 'She did tell some people he was her brother and some people he was her husband.'

Prosecutor: 'Can you tell us where various members of the family slept during that period?'

Hazel: 'Same as before, us kiddies in our tent and Mum and Harry still had the small tent.'

As Sergeant Bush concluded his questioning and took his seat, Vizzard stood up at the bar table and leant towards her over a small wooden lectern. Hazel thought the Chihuahua now looked like a vulture peering over his prey. She quickly realised that her mother and Harry's plan was to discredit her and try to show she was setting them up as some kind of revenge. It was an insult that her mother would put her through this.

Vizzard began by asking her age and how old she had been when she married Bill.

Vizzard: 'Your mother didn't want you to marry at that early age [sixteen], did she?'

Hazel: 'No. I will be twenty-four in March.'

Vizzard: 'And your mother refused to sign the papers.'

Hazel: 'No, she signed them.'

Vizzard: 'Wait until I finish … refused to sign the papers at first giving her consent to the marriage, didn't she?'

Hazel: 'Yes.'

Vizzard: 'And did you tell your mother if she didn't sign you would go away with this man?'

Hazel tried to follow Del Fricker's instructions and remain calm even though she was seething inside. Del had told her it was better to answer the questions as briefly as she could and not to get argumentative.

'No,' Hazel said.

Vizzard: 'You had not told your fiancé that you were sixteen, had you? You told him you were eighteen?'

Hazel: 'My mother had told everyone I was eighteen.'

Vizzard: 'And around 1959 you were having some arguments with your mother, weren't you?'

Hazel: '1959?'

Vizzard: 'Yes.'

Hazel: 'What sort of argument? I don't think so.'

Vizzard suggested that Hazel told someone in Sydney she had a row with her mother and was 'going to put her in' before she gave her statement to the police.

'Because I had been threatened, that is why I gave the statement,' Hazel said with a patience she didn't feel. 'I said I had come to Sydney because I had a nervous breakdown and I would give a statement to the police because I had my life threatened and my husband's and I was afraid.'

Vizzard took her briefly through her growing up, going to school in Mildura and the day her father came home in a taxi, trying to trip her up and cast doubt on her memory.

Vizzard: 'You wouldn't have a good memory of what happened when you were nine.'

Hazel: 'Some things stick out.'

The court sat right through lunch and Hazel was drained when at 2 pm, Vizzard said he had no more questions and she could leave the witness box. She sat next to Del and watched as it was Allan's turn to be grilled.

He was still living on Kangaroo Island where he had been joined by a girl he had fallen in love with, Joan, who came from way up in the north of South Australia. It had been a shock to him when Joan revealed she had six children from a previous relationship but the whole tribe had moved down to Kangaroo Island where Allan became their stepdad. By the time of the committal hearing, they had been joined by Allan and Joan's own son and daughter so there were eight kids in total.

Allan talked about the day their dad had come home from hospital.

Prosecutor: 'Was there any incident that occurred between your father and mother on that afternoon that you can recall?'

Allan: 'Yes. I can recall one instance when I remember Dad saying to Mum "I saw him kiss you". He did not mention any name. I recall Mum saying "Don't be silly, Ed, he did not".'

Vizzard was crueller to Allan than he had been to Hazel, taking advantage of their haphazard upbringing along with their lack of schooling, particularly their bad maths. Hazel thought he was downright cruel and that there was no need for it. Allan had never gone to high school, and their birthdays and even the years they were born were rarely remembered or even known in the Baron family.

Vizzard: 'Do you know how old you were at Mildura?'

Allan: 'Nine years old, as far as I remember.'

Vizzard: 'You think you were nine years old at Mildura?'

Allan: 'As far as I can remember.'

Vizzard: 'Do you know when you were born?'

Allan: 'Born? 1938.'

Vizzard: 'That would make you twelve, would it not?'

Allan: 'Perhaps it might have been twelve.'

Vizzard: 'See, you don't remember anything at all.'

Allan: 'There are a lot of things I don't remember but there are a lot of things I do remember.'

Vizzard: 'How old do you say you are now?'

Allan: 'Twenty-six.'

Vizzard: 'You are only twenty-two. Do you know that?'

Allan: 'No, I was not fully aware of that.'

Vizzard moved on to the two times Allan had been in hospital in Broken Hill, one for the accident with the horse and the other because of what he called his 'nerves'. Vizzard tried to get him mixed up with the years. It was in 1961 and 1962. Then he suddenly switched subjects, as clever and cunning barristers are trained to do during cross-examination to try to throw the witness off balance.

Vizzard must have been talking to Dulcie and Harry at length to get all this history, Hazel thought. It was yet another betrayal. She felt sorry for her brother. He gave his evidence as if he was a tape recorder, recounting conversations and answering questions in a flat voice, without emotion.

Vizzard: 'Do you drink tea?'

Allan: 'Yes.'

Vizzard: 'At Mildura?'

Allan: 'I was at Mildura, I cannot recollect. I know I have drunk tea all my life.'

Vizzard: 'All your life you have been drinking tea. You were only a little thirsty then.'

Allan: 'I would have been drinking tea then.'

Vizzard: 'You don't remember drinking tea. You just even … you don't remember drinking tea or not.'

Allan: 'I don't remember drinking tea.'

Vizzard: 'But you did drink milk when you were a little chap?'

Allan: 'That is right. I cannot remember drinking milk.'

Vizzard: 'You don't remember drinking milk either.'

Allan: 'I remember drinking milk at Mildura.'

Allan said he had never been given anything to drink when he went to bed other than cold water — except for that night his dad died when his mum gave them all hot milk and Aspros.

Vizzard: 'You have been talking to Hazel about this milk business, haven't you?'

Allan: 'I have not been talking to Hazel about that. I have not talked to her about that.'

Vizzard: 'You say Hazel has never mentioned Aspros and milk to you on any occasion?'

Allan: 'I will say that.'

After making Allan feel stupid and puzzled, Vizzard said he was finished with him.

The magistrate found that both Dulcie and Harry had a case to answer and committed them to stand trial. First they had to be arraigned and the magistrate had them both stand up in the dock. The charge was read to each of them: 'That on the thirtieth day of August 1950 in the waters of the Murray River at Buronga in the said state did feloniously and maliciously murder Edwin James Grey Baron.' Each of them said: 'I plead not guilty and reserve my defence.'

On the official court records for each of them, the court officer had scrawled 'Gaol' across the bottom, and husband and wife were taken back in separate vans to spend another miserable night apart at Long Bay.

Hazel walked outside the courthouse onto Liverpool Street, amazed to find there were still cars on the road, people walking past and the sun was still shining. So alien had it felt in the courtroom that she had forgotten about the real world. That night Del took them to the movies to help them relax but it turned into a disaster — the film was about a court case involving a husband and wife and a murder.

They walked out before the end. 'Not a good idea,' Del apologised as they left.

Hazel and Allan's involvement in the court process was far from over. The next day, Thursday, 18 February, they were joined in the courtroom by their brother Jim for the committal proceedings involving the death of Sam Overton. The Tommy Tregenza case would follow.

Three siblings all giving evidence against their mother on murder charges was unheard of.

Hazel was still protective of young Jim, despite the fact he was now aged eighteen and had recently become engaged to her husband's sister, Alma. He had been running around, kicking stones and playing hopscotch when his dad was killed, too young to hear the whispers and realise something was wrong. When Dulcie was charged with the murder of their father, Jim had been totally taken aback and broke down and wept. However, when he thought back, he had not been too surprised at the claims she had also killed Tommy and Sam Overton. Hazel was furious that Jim had been dragged into this but he took it all in his stride. In six years, he had already experienced a lifetime of knockbacks and stoicism in the shearing sheds and had learnt to pick himself up and get on with things.

Jim and Allan had been flown from Kangaroo Island to Adelaide and then to Sydney on what Jim told Hazel was the inaugural flight of a Boeing 727 between the two cities. If not the inaugural, it was certainly one of the first flights of the sleek new jet airliner which had been bought by both Trans-Australia Airlines and Ansett-ANA and it provided the brothers with a luxury they had never experienced before. They had both dressed in suits for the court case and Jim even carried a briefcase so they fitted in seamlessly with the well-heeled passengers enjoying what was then one of the best inflight services of any plane. They couldn't believe that they were served lunch in their seats.

These days, the committal hearings for the other two murders would probably not have taken place until after the trial for the murder of Ted Baron was completed. Or if they did, the evidence would have been suppressed to ensure a fair trial. Back in 1965, justice moved much quicker, a conveyor belt of murder and mayhem.

Dulcie was crying as she was led into court by a policewoman and sat alone in the dock with a handkerchief that she pressed to her forehead when she wasn't using it to wipe her eyes. The handkerchief became one of her trademark props during her court appearances.

This time Hazel figured the tears were real — a reaction to the dire situation her previously invincible mother was now in. Dulcie's whole world had fallen apart and charm and baking scones would not get her out of this. The well-constructed image that she had presented since even before Ted Baron was killed was also exposed publicly as a sham. Her previous marriage to Ted Cavanagh and the fact of her secret family was revealed to the court as the newspapers started calling her a 'mother of nine'. Police said Dulcie had told them that two of the children from her first marriage had died in a fire at Wagga Wagga. More lies.

Dulcie still couldn't understand the concept of the truth, the whole truth and nothing but the truth.

This time Vizzard reined in his sarcasm and the tricks that he had employed to make the witness he was questioning, Allan especially, look like a lying fool. The magistrate had heard it all before and there was no jury to play to. Nevertheless, he did his job well, trying to shake the testimony of the siblings, but he could not undermine the damning evidence against his client.

Dr John Laing, the New South Wales government medical officer, took the court through the evidence in his twenty-three specimen jars that showed without doubt that Sam Overton had been poisoned with arsenic. The scientific part of the case was open and shut. Overton had not died from any gastroenteritis bug.

Hazel had barely slept the night before, kept awake by the weird coincidence of the movie. Neither she nor Allan or Jim had witnessed Overton being poisoned but they were there to help the prosecution piece together the puzzle, to show motive, means and opportunity.

All three told the court that Dulcie had secured the job as Overton's cook by chasing off her predecessor with a pan of boiling water.

'She said Sam would probably not be there very long. After my mother became cook, Sam became sick,' Hazel said, recounting her visits to Netallie Station while she was working as a nurse's aide at Wilcannia Hospital.

Allan, who had been living at Netallie at the time, gave evidence about his mother asking him to kill Overton. He told the court about the time he had gone shooting ducks on the property with Overton, Dr Potts and the parish priest and how his mother had a word with him in the kitchen before they left: 'Allan, while youse are out shooting could you accidentally shoot Sam on the other side of the swamp?'

Allan said he told his mother: 'Don't be silly.'

He said that when all four of them returned uninjured, Dulcie had said to him: 'Well, at least you could have done it, Allan.'

Allan said Dulcie told Harry: 'If Sam goes, you'll be right here. He will be going.'

Vizzard could not shake their recollections and the same magistrate committed Dulcie for trial on murder two, that of Sam Overton. As it turned out, that trial would not take place until August 1967.

The court moved smoothly on to the equally horrific death of Tommy Tregenza. Jim was called as a witness because he had been sleeping in the same room as Tregenza at the Court House Hotel.

He told the court that two days before old Tommy died, his mother had told him to move into the hay shed 'to keep an eye on some things there'. It left Tregenza sleeping in the room by himself.

As Dulcie kept the handkerchief clutched to her forehead, the prosecutor asked Hazel if she had ever seen her mother make any threats against Tommy. Hazel recounted the night at the hotel when she sat down at the big table with Bill and was just about to take a spoonful of pea soup when her mother snatched the bowl away and told Hazel she was sitting in the wrong place. That was Tommy's seat! Hazel had no evidence that the soup was drugged with sleeping tablets but it had been very suspicious. Hazel also told the court that Tommy had left her mother everything in his will.

She gave evidence about how she was on duty when Tommy was brought in that night suffering critical burns and that she was there when he died the next morning.

There was one important witness the prosecution couldn't call — Hazel's friend Connie, who had been the matron and had nursed both Tommy and Sam Overton. She had died — and if Dulcie hadn't already been in jail, Hazel would have suspected her mother of being behind her death. It was Del who broke the news to Hazel that vivacious Connie, who was so full of life and such an athlete, had drowned while kayaking on Sydney Harbour. It was another blow.

The most damning evidence about Tommy's murder came in Dulcie's own words via Ray Kelly who read out her statement to the court in which she had admitted: 'Yes, I burnt him.'

Sitting in the back of the courtroom after giving her evidence, Hazel was not surprised that her mother could not look up as the police officers from Wilcannia, Sergeant Eric Madden and Constable Max Salisbury, went into the witness box. After all those comfy chats over cakes and scones in the police station, Dulcie may have thought that she had them under her spell but even if they had been taken in for a while by her friendliness, they were total professionals.

Constable Salisbury told the court how Dulcie had woken him up by knocking on his door at 2.30 am and when he got to the hotel, Tommy was badly burnt but still clinging to life.

Sergeant Madden told how Tregenza had left everything in his will to Dulcie but the will had not been valid because she had also been a signatory to it. Hazel later found out that Dulcie had been furious because the newspapers reported that she had got all his money when the truth was that she had ended up getting nothing. That's how unrealistic she was, Hazel thought. Call her a killer but not a cheat.

The police had tracked down Stanley Davis, who had employed Dulcie when he ran the Club House Hotel. Mr Davis had moved to Sydney, living in the inner-west suburb of Leichhardt, but he could still recall word for word what Dulcie had overheard Tommy telling him: 'I can afford a cup of tea, Stan. I've got two thousand pounds in the bank, eh, old mate!'

Once again, Dulcie was committed for trial and stood and told the court, as she had been advised by Vizzard: 'I plead not guilty and reserve my defence.' She was now facing three murder trials.

On top of the court hearings, Hazel and Bill had their café in Wilcannia on the market. They had decided to sell up and move to Broken Hill because Bill had lost his job. He had been working as a postie, blowing his whistle to let people know when he had put mail in their letterboxes. Most days he also drove hundreds of kilometres to customers out on their bush properties with mailboxes at the end of their private roads. The McClures at Netallie and the Fitzgeralds at Burragan were on his mail run. But Australia Post cancelled the service to save money, making people pick up their own mail when they were in town, putting Bill out of work. He had secured a job in Broken Hill at the South Mine, bringing out silver, lead and zinc. A couple of months after the committal hearings, the couple bought an old house in Broken Hill and got their first car, which they paid off on hire purchase.

In Broken Hill, Hazel finally sought medical help and was diagnosed with major depression. Hazel would never have thought of herself as suffering from a mental problem; she was the kind of person who just got on with things. However, when her condition was explained to her by the doctor, it all made sense. She had felt as though she was dragging herself through every day with a little dark grey cloud pressing down on her head. She had always been houseproud but cooking and cleaning had become a chore. Although she was struggling, she still always put the children first. She knew too well what it was like not to be cared for. Just the diagnosis helped her, because the doctor gave her hope that it was not all her fault and something could be done about it.

As was the medical custom in those days, she was given electroconvulsive therapy, ECT, better known as electric shock treatment. It was and remains a treatment almost of last resort. She discussed it with Bill and they decided it was worth trying. Hazel didn't want him to take time off work so when she had to see the psychiatrist who gave her the ECT she got the bus into town and home again. She was given a short-acting anaesthetic and muscle relaxant before electrodes placed on her scalp sent electric currents through her head, causing a brief brain seizure. The electric impulses affect the part of the brain that causes the mental problem. Altogether, she had eighteen sessions of ECT; it was a drastic treatment but coupled with antidepressant medication it helped Hazel cope. She was wrung out after her experience at the committal proceedings and had already miscarried one child because of the stress. All she wanted to do was stay at home with her young family.

Hazel was living on tenterhooks and counting the days until she had to return to face her mother again at the trial. She was also aware of how calculated Dulcie could be if she had the chance to seek revenge.

CHAPTER NINE

JUDGE AND JURY

THE TRIAL FOR THE MURDER OF TED BARON TOOK PLACE IN WHAT was still known as the 'hanging court', even though New South Wales had abolished the death penalty for murder in 1955. Hazel thought the name to be appropriate. She had never really given the death penalty much thought before, but these were wrongs that had to be righted. At that time, she truly believed her mother deserved the ultimate punishment: to hang. It wasn't very Christian, that was true, but Hazel was so bitter at all the lives Dulcie had ruined. She didn't put Harry in the same basket because she did not feel as betrayed by him as she did by her mother. As much as he was also a killer, poor weak Harry was a pathetic follower. He would have done anything for Dulcie.

Court Five, the middle court behind the columns of the old New South Wales Supreme Court off Taylor Square in Sydney's Darlinghurst, was designed with the death penalty in mind. The imposing wooden dock in the centre of the courtroom was constructed high enough off the floor so the condemned prisoner was at the same eye level as the judge up on the bench. It is the only courtroom in the state with curtains along each side of the judge. When the prisoner in the dock saw the judge pull the curtains along each side of his head from shoulder level up, they were left in no doubt about their fate. The curtains created 'blinkers' to focus the judge on the prisoner and the prisoner on the judge.

Sitting in that dock on Wednesday, 9 June 1965, were Dulcie and Harry Bodsworth. They had arrived separately in prison vans through the massive gates in the sandstone walls off Burton Street behind the court. In two of the cold cells deep under the ground, in handcuffs, they were left to sit and wait on stone benches where most of the state's notorious murderers had sat before them and would sit for years afterwards. One of the city's busiest thoroughfares, Oxford Street, passes by out the front of the courthouse but the thickness of the convict-built brick walls ensures none of the noise makes it down to the labyrinth of tunnels. Only the sound of the jailers' keys breaks the silence.

When Justice Simon Isaacs was ready to empanel the jury, the couple was led from the cells along ominous tunnels with whitewashed walls. Along the floor on each side of the tunnels run narrow channels that carried away water before proper drainage was installed. The handcuffs came off as they turned left through the solid red door with a bolt as long as a man's arm and a padlock bigger than a man's hand and walked up the surprisingly narrow wooden stairs that open up into the dock.

Those narrow silent tunnels with their brutal history would strike terror into the hearts of anyone. They had been walked by almost every one of the state's murderers since the courthouse opened in 1842, including seventy-nine who were hanged. At the other end of the tunnels was the old Darlinghurst Gaol where among those who had swung from the gallows were bushrangers such as Captain Moonlite, who was hanged in 1880, Aboriginal outlaw Jimmy Governor, hanged in 1901, and the so-called 'Black Widow' Louisa Collins, a mother of ten and the last woman to be hanged in New South Wales in 1889 for murdering her two husbands.

Guards still report hearing footsteps in the empty corridors, which are pitch black when the lights are turned out.

In the dock, Harry clasped his wife's left hand in both of his as they sat close together. Harry always needed Dulcie more than she needed him. They were on their own now, though Dulcie never really took Harry into account and felt it was her against the world. More correctly — her against the world and her daughter, Hazel. She still could not believe that Hazel had turned against her, never mind her two sons.

Hazel recalled how Dulcie had been obsessed with Jean Lee, the last woman to hang in Australia, in 1951, just six months after Ted Baron was drowned. A beautiful red-headed country girl from Dubbo, New South Wales, who had been abandoned by her drunken husband, Lee eventually fell in love with a lowlife criminal and conman, Robert David Clayton, and worked as a prostitute. Together they came up with a scam they called the 'badger game'. While she was having sex with a customer, he would burst into the room and pretend to be an outraged husband. The customer, more often than not a married man terrified of his wife finding out, would pay up. If he didn't, he had the money beaten out of him. One customer refused to pay up and was kicked and beaten to death by Clayton, Lee and their accomplice, Norman Andrews. All three were convicted of murder and sentenced to hang.

No woman had been hanged in Victoria since 1895, so the media coverage of Lee's trial and death was massive. Somewhat bizarrely, Dulcie had seen herself in Jean Lee, viewing her as a kind of romantic figure. She told Hazel that Jean Lee had been doing what she had to to look after herself and stay alive. Lee had engendered some public sympathy at the time, championed by women's groups who saw her death as a way of punishing women's immorality, of curbing the freedom and equality that women had enjoyed since the war years. Dulcie may have feared she would also be hanged, which would have been a possibility if she'd been arrested ten years earlier.

Justice Isaacs had the charges read to Dulcie and Harry before empanelling the jury. The sixty-year-old had been appointed to the bench the year before and was noted for his 'courtesy, patience, knowledge and learning'. The Prime Minister of the day, Robert Menzies, conferred upon the judge that quintessential Australian accolade of being a larrikin, labelling him a 'larrikin lawyer'.

Prosecuting the couple was Bill Knight QC, the plain-talking New South Wales Senior Crown Prosecutor, a veteran of literally hundreds of rape and murder trials in Court Five. He was a country boy from Corowa who had been the state's Senior Crown Prosecutor since 1954. His legal career had experienced only a short break when he enlisted for World War II only to be discharged thirteen days later when it was discovered he suffered from epilepsy. Before he became a prosecutor, he had built a solid reputation with a general law practice, often representing plaintiffs in negligence cases against big business, on the side of the little man in David and Goliath battles. At seventy-six, he could run prosecutions like clockwork. Just a few months earlier in the same courtroom he had prosecuted another serial killer, William MacDonald. Known as 'The Mutilator', MacDonald had murdered four men in Sydney and another in Brisbane. Most of them were homeless and were killed in city parks after MacDonald lured them into dark places, then stabbed them before slicing off their penis and testicles. Among his much-read books which were discovered by police was one on London's Jack the Ripper. He took the genitalia home and even told the jury at his trial what he then did with them before throwing them off the Sydney Harbour Bridge. It was reported that some jurors fainted and had to be taken from the court. He had pleaded insanity but the jury convicted him of murder and he was jailed for life, dying of natural causes in 2016 as the longest-serving prisoner in New South Wales.

Although Knight and Fred Vizzard were friends outside the courtroom, Vizzard would be doing him no favours when defending his client, Dulcie Bodsworth. Knight, Vizzard and Detective Ray Kelly had come up against each other in court several times, the most celebrated being the 1961 trial of Stephen Bradley for the murder of schoolboy Graeme Thorne when Knight was prosecuting and Vizzard was defending Bradley.

To avoid a conflict of interest, Harry Bodsworth was given his own counsel for the trial, the highly regarded WH Gregory, a barrister known for having a forensic eye for detail.

Crown Prosecutor Knight's opening address to the jury was succinct and to the point. As a prosecutor, it was often said he was a good defence counsel because he went into every trial aware that the Crown bore the onus of proof and if it was not there, then the accused should justifiably be acquitted.

He told the jury how Dulcie and Harry had been living in tents in Mildura when they were joined by her husband, Ted Baron, on 30 August 1950. He said Baron was drowned that same night and the Crown's case was that both the defendants had decided to kill him.

'The Crown alleges that the two accused agreed to kill Baron; and Henry Bodsworth, when Baron was asleep, carried him into the river, waded out into the water and pushed him in. He threw this sleeping man into the water.

'The motive was because they wanted to get married,' Knight said as he turned to the dock to emphasis his point by looking at the accused killers. The two had at the time been living in what he called 'an adulterous relationship'.

As do all good prosecutors, Knight took time to tell the jury about Ted Baron so the twelve men who sat in judgment could get to know him as more than a faceless 'victim'. He was a father and a husband and not just a body on a mortuary slab or, as the newspapers had reduced him to for the purposes of brevity, an 'invalid pensioner'. The jurors were told he had been in hospital for a longstanding and crippling condition of rheumatoid arthritis and needed tablets at night to sleep through the pain.

When the government medical officer, Dr James Morris, who had examined Baron's body at Wentworth, took the stand, he confirmed his finding that Baron had been alive when he went into the water because his air passages were full of fluid. In other words, he had drowned.

Then Mr Gregory, Bodsworth's counsel, rose to his feet. The defence was going to claim it could not be murder because Ted Baron had not been alive when his body was placed in the Murray River. Gregory put it to Dr Morris that he had been mistaken in his conclusion and suggested that Ted Baron had in fact already been dead 'from natural causes'. Dr Morris stuck by his report but the defence had lined up their own expert witness who would try to cast doubt on his conclusions and the prosecution case.

The defence called a Dr Brighton who was employed in the Division of Forensic Medicine of the Department of Public Health and had his own extensive experience of conducting postmortems for the coroner. Dr Brighton had not been able to examine Baron's body, even after it was exhumed, but he based his evidence on Dr Morris's report. His conclusion was that:

'The cause of death I think is not able to be determined conclusively.' He further told the jury that 'The information is just not sufficient to be positive about the actual cause of death.'

Hazel was not in court to hear this — as an upcoming witness she had to wait outside for her turn without knowing what earlier evidence was given so it would not taint what she would say.

Hazel and Bill didn't have the phone on at home and a few days earlier Hazel had received a telegram from Ray Kelly to tell her there were two tickets at Broken Hill airport for her and Bill, and that Del would meet her in Sydney where they were booked into a motel once again.

Hazel sat on the wooden bench seats outside the court, lighting cigarette after cigarette, with Del sitting on one side of her and dear Bill on the other. Allan and Jim sat nearby. Hazel was feeling clearer in her mind, after the treatment for depression, and she felt less nervous because she had already faced Dulcie three times in court already. Deep down she worried that Dulcie would be able to outsmart the jury just as she had done with people all her life. She felt that her husband had enough faith in the justice system to see both of them through.

Dr Brighton was the only independent witness that Dulcie and Harry would call in their defence. They didn't have to prove their innocence; the onus was on the prosecution to prove their guilt beyond a reasonable doubt. Their written statements to police were tendered in the trial and read to the jury, and their lawyers had to somehow counter their damaging admissions — an uphill task with officers as experienced as Ray Kelly, John Palmer and Angus Ritchie.

Just as he did with the officers who were his juniors, Kelly unfailingly treated the lawyers and the jurors with respect. He found giving evidence almost as exciting as hunting the crims because he relished sparring with the barristers and always keeping one step ahead of them. He had been in the game so long that he could predict what the next question would be, what next dark alley the lawyer would try to push him into with no way out. Kelly was able to anticipate and sidestep these stratagems, and made sure he was never cornered. Some of his colleagues thought he was a freak; he was so clever that some of the legal fraternity would go along to watch him in action.

Because Harry's defence was that Ted Baron had been dead when he put him into the water, both Kelly and Palmer were cross-examined about the part of Harry's statement where he said that there had been a bit of a scuffle with Baron. It was put to them that they had in fact asked Harry if Baron had been breathing and that Harry had told them: 'No, he was dead'. Kelly said simply that those words had never been said.

Palmer said he could not remember whether they had asked Harry whether Baron had made any movement or cried out and denied that he had asked Harry whether Baron was breathing or if he did anything to show he was alive.

The prosecution understood that Hazel needed to get home to the kids so they called her as the next witness. She was wearing her favourite double string of pearls again. She didn't have many fancy clothes but she knew that making an effort for the jury was more important than it had been in the committal proceedings. As her turn came and she walked through the heavy wooden doors into Court Five, everything seemed heightened, sharpened, on the edge: the sound of her footsteps as she walked to the witness box, the voice of the judge's associate as he asked her to take the oath on the Bible, even the eyes of everyone in the courtroom on her. It was as if she could hear them watching her.

She made a point of looking straight at her mother, who was wearing the same green suit as she had at the committal. Hazel saw a woman who looked broken. She didn't for a moment believe that her mother was actually 'broken' — Dulcie was merely putting on a good act. Hazel knew she was as wicked as ever.

In answers to questions from Bill Knight, Hazel said her father had seemed in good spirits when he came home that last day from the hospital and told how her mum had given the kids Aspros to help them sleep. She revealed the cruel burden of secrets that Dulcie had placed upon her young family to keep her relationship with Harry a secret from their father.

Knight: 'Can you recall whether your mother spoke to you in Mildura as to what you were to tell your father if he asked anything about the life in Mildura?'

Hazel: 'Yes … she just told us not to say that she had been sleeping with Harry and that he had been just looking after us. He took us to Mildura and he had just been looking after us and that was about all.'

After she gave her evidence in chief, Vizzard, the snapping Chihuahua, asked the same question he had asked her during the committal hearing: 'Mrs Baron, have you ever told a lie? Yes or no.'

Hazel was twenty-four but felt like a ten-year-old about to be scolded by a parent. She was angry about this and it sparked a realisation that she was stronger than she thought. The memory of the last day she saw her dad flashed into her mind; the tall, handsome man leaning on a stick, smiling as he walked towards their tents while Toby the terrier ran circles of joy around his feet. She thought about Harry holding her father under the water until he died. Neither Ted nor the dog were there now but Hazel was and she felt she owed it to both of them to keep it together and not let her mother win.

With a strength within her that she didn't know was there, she answered: 'Yes.' She couldn't bring herself to look at the jury sitting to her right but she figured that not one of them would have been able to answer that trick question any differently. She would not let this theatrical lawyer goad her and she refused to be rattled. It was the jury whose trust she had to win, no one else's. She kept her voice steady as she answered all the rest of his questions during cross-examination, which differed little from what Vizzard had already asked in the Magistrates Court.

Jim was as calm as ever and Allan had also got over some of his nervousness and timidity. Hazel watched from the public benches as they gave their evidence and she felt proud of her little brothers. None of them wanted to hang around waiting to hear what their mother and stepfather had to say for themselves. Hazel and Bill flew back to Broken Hill as soon as they could on the next flight out of Sydney, while Allan and Jim went back to Adelaide and then Kangaroo Island. They felt like they had been holding their breath for the past three days and couldn't wait to get back to the bush and breathe in the hot outback air, unpolluted by city bullshit.

Dulcie and Harry had three choices. The first was to say nothing, but their lawyers advised them that such a course of action never went down well with a jury. No matter how much they were told that the accused did not have to prove their innocence, jurors always thought that a defendant who said nothing had something to hide. The second was to go into the witness box, give evidence on oath and face the onslaught of cross-examination by the prosecutor. Both Vizzard and Gregory knew that their clients were not the most eloquent and educated of people. Dulcie might have been able to pull it off with her cunning, but not Harry. The defence team was aware of how quickly he had folded when spoken to by police and that was without the pressure of withering questioning. They could not have one defendant go into the witness box and not the other, so it was never an option that was seriously considered by the defence team. The third was to deliver an unsworn statement that turned the dock into what was known as 'coward's castle', because they could state their case without being questioned on it. The police called it a licence to lie.

Bizarrely, as the law stood at the time, jurors could not be told that defendants had those three choices available to them. In the case of the third option, even if the jury came back with a question during their deliberations seeking to clarify why all the other witnesses had been cross-examined and not the defendants, the judge was not allowed to explain it to them. Nor could the defendant be charged with perjury. Essentially, an unsworn statement gave them a free kick. No wonder it was called 'coward's castle'. It was an anomaly in the justice system that has since been removed by law, but it was the course chosen by both Dulcie and Harry. They had been advised by their lawyers to be brief and not to ramble. Both had rehearsed their statements before they stood up in the dock.

Harry went first. He faced the jury, as his barrister had advised him to do, and looked along them, from man to man. He pulled himself up straight and tried to project a confident air. He spoke slowly if not eloquently.

'I know I done wrong when I put Baron's body in the river, but he was dead before I went into his tent that night.

'When I went in he was not breathing. I had a good look; there was a sort of Tilley light above the bed. It was cold and you could see your breath coming out and there was none coming out of him. The first thing I saw was there was no rising and falling in the blankets, no breathing. I had a good look and there was no breath coming out of his nose or mouth.'

As he spoke, Dulcie had her handkerchief out and was dabbing her eyes behind her thick-lensed glasses with their dark frames that made her face look severe and older than her 'fifty-one' years, which of course she was — five years older. Those five years she had got rid of way back when she married Ted Baron had never been rediscovered, not by the police nor by the justice system, and Dulcie certainly wasn't going to put them right. When Hazel saw her mother's age reported in the newspapers as 'fifty-one' she just laughed. Dulcie had several dates of birth. One of her favourites had been 1912 because she liked to tell people she had been 'born in the same year the *Titanic* sank'. It made a good story.

'Mr Kelly and Mr Palmer both asked me in Melbourne was there any breathing or whether he had done anything to show he was alive or cry out. I answered "no" to this question. He didn't, he was dead. I panicked and put him in the river,' he said.

'I love Dulcie and I love her now. He was dead when I put him in the river and I didn't do anything to cause that.'

Then Dulcie stood, twisting her handkerchief in both hands down by her stomach as she spoke. Like Harry, her version of events was truncated. She said she had met Harry in Wangaratta and they had 'become friendly'.

'My husband came to Wangaratta but I did not live with him as husband and wife. He was taken to hospital and I used to visit him every afternoon. After he came out I told him I was going to leave Wangaratta and he would have to get board,' she said.

'I took him to a boarding house and got his board and he came back to ask my son and daughter if they wanted to stay with him. They said they would go with Mum and then my friend Bodsworth said he would come with me.

'We came to Mildura and I wrote to Baron that the children were all right and we were happy and not to worry about us. Next thing I got a wire to say he was coming over.

'I met him at the bus stop and took him home but after a short time he went to hospital again with arthritis. He came home about 31 August — I would not like to say just the date now, it was so many years ago. I told him it was too cold in the tent. He was quite normal and well only for the arthritis in his hands.

'That afternoon we walked around and we had tea and he went to bed. I went up to the little shop on the corner, got what I wanted for the next morning, came back and went to bed.

'I never saw Bodsworth then but I went out later in the night to the toilet. As I was going past I said "Are you home, Harry?" and he said "Yes". When I came back Bodsworth met me and told me he had pushed my husband in the river.

'I said to him "Whatever will we do? We will just have to tell". Bodsworth said "No. Forget all about it."

'I said "We will have to tell" and he put his arm around me and said "No". At no time was it discussed to push Baron in the river.

'Bodsworth has been a good husband and stepfather. I had an interview with Inspector Kelly and he told me that Bosworth had admitted all he had done.'

By the end of the second day, Thursday, Hazel and Bill were home, all the witnesses had been heard and the lawyers had begun their addresses to the jury in which they summed up their clients' cases. Dulcie's defence was simple — she didn't know anything about what Harry had done until it was all over. Harry's statement, however, created a quandary for Justice Isaacs and he made a decision that would come back to haunt the judge.

Gregory's argument was that his client could not be found guilty of murder because even if the jury was satisfied that Ted

Baron had been alive when he was pushed into the river and had drowned, they had to have regard to what Harry had told them — that he had formed the opinion that Baron was already dead when he carried him from the tent. His defence was that he had made a mistake, a bona fide mistake, by believing Baron was dead so 'then it is not murder because it was not done with malice'.

The prosecution put that down as silly and a 'fantastic' suggestion. Justice Isaacs expressed his puzzlement as to what it actually meant and, more importantly, how he should instruct the jurors regarding what it meant when they retired to consider their verdict.

In the absence of the jury, he asked both the defence and the prosecution if such an argument meant they wanted him to instruct the jury that they could find Harry not guilty of murder but guilty to the lesser crime of manslaughter. He said that he believed that being mistaken that someone was dead before burying them — in the ground or in the water — was not a defence to murder but it might be enough to reduce the crime to manslaughter. Both the defence and the prosecution said they wanted the jury left with only the two choices — guilty of murder or not guilty of murder.

Sometimes even the best judges can trip up over their own words. When it came to instructing the jury, Justice Isaacs told them very carefully that in his opinion, there was no evidence on which they could return a verdict of manslaughter: 'You are at liberty to disregard it; you are at liberty to disagree with it. That is all I propose to say in respect of that matter; it is a matter for you.'

He also told the jury that Harry bore the onus of proof to show that he truly believed Ted Baron was already dead, although he only had to prove it to the civil test of 'on the balance of probabilities' while the prosecution still had to prove his guilt to the criminal level of 'beyond reasonable doubt'.

Late in the morning of Friday, 11 June, the jury finally retired to the jury room to consider its verdict. Dulcie and Harry were led back down the narrow wooden stairs from the dock and handcuffed before being taken to separate cells where they could talk to each other but not touch each other. Just one and three-quarter hours later, the jury had made up its mind.

Dulcie and Harry stood in the dock as the jurors filed back into the room.

In the wooden benches reserved for the police, Kelly, Palmer and Ritchie were pretty confident that the jury would find both of them guilty. They felt that the testimony of the witnesses, particularly that given by Hazel and Allan, had been powerful — but you could never be sure. The history of wins and losses was etched into the varnished wood of the benches where past and present detectives had scratched their names and the names of their trials. That was the good — and bad — of the jury system. You take twelve people who had probably never been in a courtroom before and while the police try to make the case as straightforward as possible, the lawyers try to baffle them with convoluted arguments.

Justice Isaacs asked the foreman of the jury to stand before he delivered the unanimous verdicts: guilty to each charge of murder. The tears Dulcie had shed over the previous two days had dried up and the newspapers reported that neither she nor Harry showed any emotion as they learnt their fate.

The judge discharged the jury but most of the jurors stayed behind in the public seats at the back of the court to see what was going to happen. Despite the 'sexual revolution' taking place everywhere else, in the Australia of the early sixties a woman's place was still considered to be in the kitchen and not the dock of a courtroom. It was a bit of a novelty for a woman to be convicted of murder.

No accused murderers made it to trial in New South Wales in those days without meeting the eccentric Dr Oscar Schmalzbach. Schmalzbach was a Polish Jew who had escaped the Nazis through Romania to make Australia his home. As one of the first forensic psychiatrists in New South Wales to be used regularly by the police and the prosecution, he was a bit of a legend, if both chaotic and imperious in his private life and sometimes in the evidence he gave in court. He enjoyed driving out to the jails to interview fresh subjects and sat down no fewer than three times with Dulcie and twice with Harry separately. The main reason was to ascertain that they were both fit to plead and Schmalzbach reported that neither suffered from any mental illness.

The report he prepared for Harry was straightforward, containing an accurate family background as related by Harry, and concluded: 'He is fit to plead and to follow his trial intelligently.'

The report on Dulcie was more of a work of art — her art, not the good doctor's — as she mixed fact and fiction about her past. She claimed that after her first marriage, she took the couple's two daughters and left the two boys with their father. A lie. She described her second husband, Ted Baron, as cruel. Another lie.

Then she tried to engender sympathy by talking about how she suffered for her work ethic: 'She said that she did suffer from dizzy spells and feelings of fainting and the doctors ... have told her that she worked too hard. She has been suffering from terrible headaches for which on some occasions she has been taking twelve Bex powders per day, apart from taking other similar tablets for years.'

His report on Dulcie indicated that she had impressed the psychiatrist as a 'simple person of little education', when in truth she would have been one of the most complex killers he had ever met. His job, however, had not been to provide an in-depth examination.

Dr Schmalzbach's reports made it onto the record before Justice Isaacs sentenced Dulcie and Harry that same day. He told them to stand. Harry gripped Dulcie's left hand in both of his.

'There is only one penalty which the law imposes for this finding,' he told them.

'You are each sentenced to imprisonment for life.'

It had been worth the jurors staying. Dulcie Bodsworth became the first woman to be sentenced for life in New South Wales in seven years.

The first thing Ray Kelly did — even before repairing to the pub for a few celebratory drinks — was to send a cryptic telegram to Hazel in Broken Hill: 'Saw mother today. It seems like a lifetime.' Hazel knew what he meant in their secret code, which stopped the telegram people from gossiping.

At first she felt relief. Relief that Dulcie could not kill anyone else and relief because she could now feel safe with her mother locked away for a number of years. But that night after she had tucked in the kids and got into bed, her feelings turned to sadness. She imagined her mother with a cell door slammed shut behind her and the light turned off, and she hoped she would be treated well. Despite it all, Hazel could not turn off her feelings towards her mother. And despite feeling that her mother deserved the death penalty, she knew she could never have lived with herself had that actually happened. She usually slept like a log but that night she lay awake as she tried to process her emotions which were in turmoil.

She could draw no comfort by looking back at the past. Their childhoods had been difficult and unsettled, and force of will would not bring back her father — or Sam Overton or Tommy Tregenza. She could find no empathy for Dulcie and nor could she feel sorry for her. Normal people didn't do what she had done and Dulcie had never cared about anyone but herself. Hazel thought:

Why should I care about her? Despite it all, though, she did care, but she never regretted going to the police and giving evidence. She knew she had done the right thing.

Allan wasn't as tough as Hazel and he took to drinking. He had kept so much of his past bottled up for so long and he felt like a bastard for putting his mother away, while at the same time he had, like Hazel, wanted her to hang for what she had put them all through. They were all too aware that, even though they were adults, Dulcie could still both rule and ruin their lives.

CHAPTER TEN

MARGARET AND ALLAN BARON

THEN DULCIE AND HARRY APPEALED.

It meant the trial for the murder of Tommy Tregenza, scheduled for later in 1965, had to be put on hold. Police had been unable to find any relatives of the old man to let them know. He had died homeless and alone just as he had lived much of his life homeless and alone. He had not married and had no known children. His mother Bridget had died in 1895 when Tommy was just seven; his father Robert didn't marry again and died in 1918. Among the other Tregenzas who had lived at Naracoorte and helped bring up Tommy, there was no one who really remembered their cousin and uncle.

In Adelaide, Sam Overton's widow Margaret, their son David and her family the McClures, who owned Netallie Station, were on tenterhooks waiting for their trial to be held so they could begin to put Sam's death behind them. David, who was twenty-three and the spitting image of his dad, had relied on his uncles while growing up without a father. David had recently met the girl he would marry two years down the track. The Overton murder trial had been scheduled for early 1966, after the Tregenza trial. Now, it too was put on hold pending the outcome of the appeal.

The two charges of arson which had been laid against Dulcie had gone on the back burner. They had been brought really so police could arrest her and keep her in custody while they questioned her about the murders. At Burragan Station, old Madge Fitzgerald and her daughter Lin had rebuilt the barn and homestead that Dulcie had burnt down. Building in the bush was a mammoth task with most materials having to come from as far away as Broken Hill at least and often further. Mother and daughter had lived in the two-bedroom cottage for over a year before the new house was habitable. Police kept them up to date with what was happening with Dulcie but made it clear that they would press ahead with the arson charges only if Dulcie was cleared of all the murders.

Thus the lives of all those families, as well as the lives of Hazel, Allan and their little brother Jim, were up in the air while the Bodsworths argued they had been wrongly convicted.

All judges have to be assessed by their peers as well as by the public, and Justice Simon Isaacs had realised after the trial for the murder of Ted Baron that he had made a mistake in his instructions to the jury. The Court of Criminal Appeal said as much in its judgment that quashed the Bodsworths' convictions and ordered the couple face a new trial. There were a number of grounds of appeal but the main reason for the appeal court's decision was because Justice Isaacs had got it wrong when he reversed the onus of proof from the prosecution onto Harry's defence to show that he believed Ted Baron was already dead when he pushed him out into the deep water. The onus of proof is never on the defendant; it had been on the Crown to prove that Baron had been alive, not on Harry to prove that he thought he was dead.

The jury may well have come to the same guilty decision had Justice Isaacs not made that mistake, but such are the workings of the law. The jury is not consulted. Hazel thought this was silly but she didn't try to understand it all.

On 16 December 1965, she got another of Ray Kelly's cryptic telegrams: 'Saw mother today and she won.' It meant she had won the appeal. Hazel was gutted. It was not a good Christmas present. She wondered if it had been worth coming forward in the first place. She was no longer scared of her mother physically but mentally she felt much safer with her behind bars.

Three days after the Court of Criminal Appeal handed down its ruling, Ronald Ryan and Peter Walker escaped from Pentridge jail only to be captured by Ray Kelly and the indomitable Del Fricker in Sydney after nineteen days on the run. Hazel, a paper-holic and news-aholic, read every word in the newspapers about the woman who had become one of her heroes. She felt proud to know her.

Hazel and Bill along with their daughter and adopted son had somewhat reluctantly settled into life in Broken Hill. The city would never be as busy as it was around that time when its population reached a high of around 30,000. Their three-bedroom single-storey house in Bagot Street felt like it was in suburbia compared to the openness of Wilcannia. The house was typical of the town at that time, a 'starter' home built in 1945 in neat rows by the government as part of its deal with the mining company Broken Hill Proprietary Ltd (which became the 'Big Australian' BHP) to develop the town and support the local industry. It had been added on to since then, with a car port and such, and the first thing Hazel did was fill the garden beds with her favourite zinnias.

Hazel's reluctance was because although she loved the desolate landscape — the clear blue skies that went on forever, the smell of the desert and life in the bush — she never felt at ease with the way the unions ran the town. It seemed like a hardworking laid-back sort of place but it was very territorial. Hazel wasn't political at all but she did appreciate all the unions had done to make the inherently dangerous business of mining much safer and how they had fought for eight-hour days instead of 72-hour weeks. But she did not like bullies — bullies who could ruin the business of a popular local butcher just because he had bought his meat from the 'wrong' farmer. Camaraderie and mateship were all to the good but it was not fair that in 1965, anyone who bought from a black banned business could expect to be frozen out and even lose their job. She wished she had been as brave as one of her friends who had walked through the picket line into that butcher's shop, telling them they could all 'fuck off', and bought meat from him. That woman could be brave: her husband didn't work at the mines, and her gesture wouldn't affect his livelihood.

Hazel was once again able to love making her house into a home so she could wrap her little family in it like a blanket to keep them safe in a way that she had never felt while growing up. She couldn't have worked even if she wanted to because she saw how jobs were given to men and single women first, and married women pite a proud history of backing their men during the years of devastating industrial battles — were expected to stay home. She did a few shifts helping at the local hospital when they were shorthanded and took on a bit of house cleaning for extra money.

While Hazel and her brothers were fretting about whether they had to give evidence again in the retrial for the murder of their father, the news arrived that Dulcie and Harry were going to plead not guilty to murder but they would plead guilty to the manslaughter of Ted Baron in a deal with the prosecution to avoid another trial. Bill Knight agreed to the course of action and on 1 March 1966, the couple was back in the dock at Court Five.

Justice John Henry 'Jock' McClemens had spent fifteen years sitting on some of the toughest civil and criminal trials and appeals in the state and was known for sometimes showing too much sympathy towards defendants. But this case had him floored.

'The circumstances are without parallel,' he said.

'All the circumstances surrounding this are so bizarre. Here is a woman with eight children with two men, one her husband. Then she enters into an agreement with Bodsworth to kill her husband by whom she had had four children. Bosworth was twenty-two and she was thirty-seven.' (Still no one had picked up on Dulcie's real age.)

'Then they have thirteen years of married life together and another child.'

The judge said he was under no illusion who was the instigator of the killing. Despite Dulcie's denials to have known nothing about her lover's evil plan, the judge knew who wore the pants in their relationship.

'I have read statements made by both of these people and have formed the impression that Bodsworth was under the domination of Mrs Baron,' Justice McClemens said, which seemed to belie the prosecution's decision to accept the couple's plea of guilty to manslaughter instead of pressing ahead with a murder trial.

He said that so much disturbed him about the case that he refused to pass sentence without a 'complete psychiatric report'. He adjourned the appeal for three weeks.

In the dock and still in love with the woman who was the most exciting person he had ever met even if she had ruined his life, Harry demonstrated once more that he did not mind being 'dominated'. He tenderly held his wife's left hand, and as she rose to leave the court, he stepped forward and kissed her full on the lips. Justice McClemens granted a request for them to see each other in the cells below the court before they were taken back to jail.

Hazel couldn't believe the schmaltz when she read it in the next day's newspapers. She wanted to vomit.

Psychiatric reports again found that neither of them had any mental problems. When the Bodsworths came back before the judge on 24 March, speaking up for them was the former Baptist minister from Hopetoun, the Reverend WG Embury, who described the couple as 'highly respected'. What a shock the Reverend Embury got when he heard the whole truth.

'This matter has caused me grave concern because the case is so unusual,' Justice McClemens told Dulcie and Harry, who had by then become a laughing stock among the reporters as they persisted in holding hands in the dock while sitting with pathetic looks on their faces.

'A man has died because he stood in the way of your association. His only crime was that he was in your way.'

Again the judge singled out Dulcie.

'Baron used to take sleeping tablets and slept very soundly. She walked away while Bodsworth carried Baron to the river and pushed him in,' he said.

'On any showing, this is a very serious crime and the lowest sentence I can impose is five years.'

Justice McClemens said he had taken into account their age and that it appeared they had spent many years happily together and were useful members of the community, although he acknowledged Dulcie was facing other murder charges.

Five years. The detectives thought that both Dulcie and Harry had got off easy and worried how it would affect Hazel. 'Saw mother today and she got five', Kelly said in the latest telegram to her.

Hazel was furious. What had happened to life behind bars? She thought about the word 'manslaughter' and realised it could be broken down into two words: mans-laughter. She had done the right thing going to the police but the justice system had let her down, let her father down. Dulcie must be laughing at putting one over on them. Ted Baron's life was worth only five years. It was a joke in her eyes. Dulcie and Harry had killed her father and she vowed to herself to do her best to get her mother convicted of murder next time.

As Dulcie's trial for the murder of Tommy Tregenza approached, Hazel put herself through the wringer. There were times when she blamed herself for the old man's death. She had had no control over her father's drowning nor the poisoning of Sam Overton but should she have alerted Tommy and the police when she saw the same warning signs?

Dulcie had given indications of her sinister plan before Overton's murder, talking about him drinking heavily. Then she had almost predicted Tommy's death, voicing her 'worries' about him smoking in bed and falling asleep in one of his drunken stupors and setting himself on fire. Hazel had also feared that her mother was putting sleeping tablets in Tommy's soup at dinner. If only she had had the guts to tell someone, but who would have listened to her? She felt she would have been treated as little more than a kid and kids make up stories — that's what they would have put it down to. The what-ifs caused Hazel a lot of despair.

She had known that Tommy was a loner, but when the police told her that he had had no choice because he had actually been all alone, with no family, Hazel cried. She realised that was one of the reasons he liked a drink because when you are drinking in a bar, no one is alone and everyone is your friend.

*

The weather always seemed harder in Sydney. The harsh grey of the buildings made it appear hotter in the summer and colder in the winter. On a miserable overcast Thursday in the late winter of 1966, Hazel and Jim were back in Court Five to face their mother yet again. When she heard the trial for Tommy's murder was set down for August, Hazel had prayed it would be over before 30 August, the anniversary of her father's death. It was. The trial only took two days, 18 and 19 August. Despite her misgivings, it seemed to fly past. Now, they just needed to await the verdict.

Jim told Hazel that he was moving to Broken Hill where he had secured a job at the North Mine, and that he and Alma were planning on getting married in the same church in Wilcannia where Hazel and Bill had wed.

Allan and Joan were also leaving Kangaroo Island and moving to Olary Station, a sheep property outside the small settlement of Olary way up in the north of South Australia, right next to the state's eastern boundary and close to where Joan came from. He was going to work again as a station hand. Hazel's head was spinning and she was delighted at the news that all the family, except for Margaret, would be close together again.

Ray Kelly had retired from the police in February that year with a massive farewell dinner at Sydney's ritzy Chevron Hotel. In Potts Point, it had been hailed as the city's 'First International Hotel' when it opened in 1960, hosting glamorous guests of the calibre of Ella Fitzgerald, Shirley Bassey and the Bee Gees. It banned the Beatles because of the 'annoying' screaming crowds the Fab Four attracted everywhere they went. Kelly was going to go out with a bang as spectacular as his career and there were reportedly 874 guests at five pounds a head, which included a table of food and all they could drink. The New South Wales Premier of the day, Robert Askin, described him as a close personal friend and told the packed room that no fictional detective could hold a candle to his mate. In 1975, Kelly was awarded the MBE after successful lobbying by Askin.

The prosecution case in Tommy Tregenza's trial had been much more straightforward than it had been in Ted Baron's. There was no dispute over Tommy's cause of death and the jury heard that the former jockey had suffered burns to a horrifying seventy-two per cent of his body. The stalwart prosecutor Bill Knight declared the motive was financial because Tregenza had left Dulcie 600 pounds in his will — all he had in the world.

Despite his retirement, Kelly was at court to support Hazel and also to give evidence about the confession Dulcie had made to police at Melbourne police headquarters in Russell Street almost two years earlier. It was one of his few cases still unresolved since leaving the force.

Dulcie's damning police interview was read to the jury.

Kelly: 'Did you have anything to do with the death of Tommy Tregenza?'

Dulcie: 'Yes, I did, I burnt him. I put a match on his bed.'

Kelly: 'Bed clothes would not ignite in a way they did in this room unless there was some inflammable substance present. Did you place anything or pour anything in the bed?'

Dulcie: 'Yes, methylated spirits.'

Kelly: 'Where did you get the methylated spirits from?'

Dulcie: 'I had it in my bedroom; I always rub my legs with it.'

Hazel felt it easier to give evidence against her mother this time. She felt an icy calmness as she looked up at her from the witness box. Dulcie was wearing that same green suit which Hazel had come to think of as her 'court uniform'. Jim once again took it all in his stride and both siblings gave the same evidence that they had done at the committal hearing.

Dulcie's new barrister, John Atwill, was the total opposite of the Chihuahua-like Vizzard. Unlike the diminutive public defender, Atwill, whose name in full was the grand-sounding Milton John Napier Atwill, was just as he was described in newspapers of the time: 'tall, handsome and poised'. Looking back, Hazel thought he resembled George Clooney. His style of cross-examination was no less thorough than that of Vizzard but he acted without the sarcasm, possibly because he came from the private bar and not all of his work was in the cut-throat business of criminal trials. The self-assured Atwill went on to become the federal president of the Liberal Party and in 1978 he became Sir Milton John Napier Atwill after being knighted by the Queen.

Hazel and Jim had flown into Sydney on the Wednesday and were on their way home before Sergeant Eric Madden and Constable Max Salisbury and Stan Davis, the former licensee of Wilcannia's Club House Hotel where Tommy had stayed before Dulcie got her claws into him, gave evidence.

Once again, after being advised against going into the witness box by her barrister, Dulcie chose to remain in 'coward's castle' and make a safe statement from the dock. She had no one's hand to hold this time, being all alone, but the detectives thought she had grown in confidence after her win in overturning her earlier murder conviction. She stood and told the jury that she had been in bed with her husband on the night Tregenza died. Her husband had woken her up and said there was something glaring on the window. He had jumped out of bed and run outside, saw that Tregenza's bedroom was on fire and asked Dulcie to go for help.

She said she had never 'done the old man any harm' and, indeed, on a former occasion had found him asleep in an armchair with a pillow burning and had woken him up.

'At no time did I ever wish Tregenza any harm or do such a thing,' she said.

'Regarding the will, the old chap brought in a piece of paper and asked me to sign my name on it, which I did, and he left immediately afterwards.'

Dulcie said that she had offered Tregenza a bowl of soup for supper that night but he had declined, then he had 'got some drink in a bottle' and it was the last time she had seen him.

Dulcie did not deny her confession to police but explained it away by saying that she had been so distressed at that time that she would have told them anything.

Usually juries are just seen, and only heard when they raise questions after retiring to consider their verdict. But as Atwill closed the defence case and Dulcie sat down, the foreman of the jury rose to his feet. The lawyers looked at each other, the detectives shuffled in their seats. This was almost unheard of. No one had any idea what the man was going to ask.

He raised the elephant in the room — where was Harry? He said the jury wanted to know why Harry hadn't been called to give evidence: 'Is there any reasonable explanation why there has been no statement from the husband or any evidence from the husband?'

The prosecution couldn't call Harry because a husband could not be compelled to give evidence against his wife. While it was open to the defence to call him, his evidence would not have helped them — he had been there when Dulcie admitted to having set Tommy's bed on fire. Furthermore, putting him in the witness box would have opened him up to being cross-examined by the Crown.

When it came to summing up the case for the jury, the trial judge, Justice PH Allen, explained Harry's absence in simple, straightforward terms. He told the jury that if the defence had not called the husband, then the defence was entitled to explain why not.

'[And] if no explanation is offered and none given, it is an inference open to a jury that the testimony of that witness could probably not assist the party who fails to call such a witness, and I should add that there is no rule of law which prevents an accused woman from calling as a witness her own husband on any aspect of the case if it wished to do so,' Justice Allen said.

But, as had Justice Isaacs in the earlier trial involving Ted Baron, Justice Allen had got it wrong. He realised not long after the words were out of his mouth that he had made a mistake.

The law was that the failure of an accused person, or the wife or husband of an accused person, to give evidence could never be made the subject of any comment by the judge or by either the prosecution or the defence. Justice Allen tried to correct his error by telling the jury that he withdrew what he had said earlier and they should 'completely disabuse their minds' of his remarks. It was like telling them to forget that someone had admitted to murder.

When the jury had retired to consider the verdict, the judge offered to discharge the jury and start again. Bill Knight said he would 'not object' to that course of action but Atwill said he had consulted with his client and they had decided not to apply for the jury to be discharged. These were all tactical steps designed to give them appeal points should the jury return a guilty verdict.

Which it did. In those days it was usual for juries to continue deliberations in the jury room after the court's usual sitting hours ended at 4 pm. This Friday night, the court sat back. After deliberating for a couple of hours, the jury returned with its verdict. Dulcie Bodsworth was guilty of murdering Tommy Tregenza. The judge did not hesitate to sentence her to life.

Ray Kelly's telegram reached Hazel the next day: 'Saw mother today. It seems like a lifetime.'

But Hazel's relief was once again short-lived. Dulcie appealed and her conviction was overturned because of the judge's mistake. It was telling, however, that the Court of Criminal Appeal did so reluctantly, saying the law was old-fashioned regarding husbands and wives giving evidence against each other: 'I say this with some regret because a new trial of criminal proceedings should be avoided where possible. There should be an end to criminal litigation and it is in the interests of justice that this should be so but when the court is faced with an appeal such as Mr Atwill has made to set aside this verdict of guilty, we cannot do other than accede to it.'

Hazel and Jim never even made it into the witness box when the retrial was held in February the following year, 1967. Atwill, who was again representing Dulcie, objected to Ray Kelly reading out her police record of interview, arguing it had not been made 'freely and voluntarily' because she had been 'coerced' by Harry. The latest judge, the highly respected Justice Robert Taylor, rejected the tender of the police statement and directed the jury to acquit Dulcie. They did so, and that was that. Hazel felt as though the justice system had let her and Tommy down.

Justice Taylor was certainly no bleeding heart, although that did nothing to appease Hazel. Just six years later he presided over the horrific rape and murder trial of Allan Baker and Kevin Crump. Career criminals who had met in jail, their first victim was itinerant worker Ian Lamb, shot dead while sleeping in his car in a thrill-kill on 3 November 1973. They didn't even know him.

Five days later they notoriously abducted mother-of-three Virginia Morse, thirty-five, from her family property in western New South Wales. Over the next few days, they repeatedly raped and tortured her until they shot her dead just over the Queensland border. The full shocking details of her final hours have never been revealed. Justice Taylor's words to Baker and Crump when he sentenced them for life continue to reverberate: 'You have outraged all accepted standards of the behaviour of men. The description of "men" ill becomes you. You would be more aptly described as animals, and obscene animals at that. I believe that you should spend the rest of your lives in gaol and there you should die. If ever there was a case where life imprisonment should mean what it says — imprisonment for the whole of your lives — this is it.'

*

As the Baron siblings counted down to what they hoped would be the final time they would have to give evidence — in the trial over the murder of Sam Overton — their lives were rocked by another tragedy.

The Overton trial was due to begin on 21 August 1967. On 16 August, the same day that Hazel, Allan and Jim received their letters from the police along with their plane tickets to Sydney, they got the news that their sister Margaret had died. She was twenty-three, married to a farmer, and her death came suddenly from a cyst on the brain.

Hazel was sad that she and Margaret had lost touch after she moved to Hopetoun with Dulcie and Harry. She heard news of her through Jim but felt it was too dangerous to write to her while the police were gathering evidence against Dulcie and Harry. Hazel felt she couldn't trust anyone, not even her own sister.

Hazel got her address from Jim and wrote to her after their mother was arrested. Margaret had been both angry and devastated. She didn't believe Dulcie or Harry could kill anyone. But slowly she had come to realise it was true and their convictions for her father's drowning had come as a shock. She had been suffering headaches and visited the doctor as they got worse but the doctor put it down to 'nerves' because of the murder. Margaret was another of Dulcie's victims, Hazel thought.

She left behind a twenty-month-old baby. The families drove to Hopetoun for what was a heartbreaking funeral.

Hazel had let Ray Kelly know and he told her that Dulcie could demand permission to attend her daughter's funeral, escorted by police. It was something Hazel couldn't even begin to cope with so she asked Kelly not to tell her mother. It was a decision she never agonised about. The families got back to Broken Hill on 19 August to find that three days after Jim's twin sister had died, his wife Alma was in hospital to give birth to their second child.

They felt as though they had been caught in a whirlwind, a tornado that had picked them up from the ground, was spinning them around and wouldn't let go. The next day, 20 August, the three siblings flew to Sydney to give evidence against their mother over the death of Sam Overton. Hazel was so upset about Margaret's death and consumed with worry about Margaret's child and Jim and Alma's baby that she could hardly think. Years later she could recall little of the trial and even forgot that Jim had given evidence.

Outside court, Sam Overton's widow, Margaret Overton, put her arms around Hazel and gave her a warm hug.

'You poor kids, what you must have gone through,' she said.

At the very time Hazel felt she should have been the one consoling Mrs Overton, the Adelaide nurse's words and actions brought Hazel comfort. At that moment, Margaret Overton was like the mother Hazel never had. Dulcie had never hugged her with a mother's love and selflessness.

When she faced her mother in court this time, Hazel sensed fresh venom. It wasn't something anyone else in the courtroom could have seen; it was just the look in Dulcie's eyes. Hazel could guess why. She had found out that at the exact time Margaret's funeral began, at 3 pm, a doctor at Long Bay went with a prison warder to break the news to Dulcie. They told Hazel that Dulcie had 'performed a real treat', demanding to go, there and then, professing her innocence of everything and threatening that if anyone else died, she would sue Hazel if she wasn't told about it.

Who else was going to die? Hazel thought.

She found out much later that Dulcie had been smuggling letters out of jail to Allan asking him to retract his evidence and saying things like: 'How could you say that when I gave birth to you?' He struggled against her vitriol and felt really bad for trying to get his mother locked up for life.

For Hazel, it was reassuring to see the familiar face of Bill Knight prosecuting again and to have Del Fricker back at her side for support. The George Clooney lookalike Atwill was again representing Dulcie.

The defence could not argue with Overton's cause of death — the amount of arsenic in his coffin was overwhelming. The poison had caused him to suffer a slow torture and an excruciating death. Their only chance was to cast doubt in the jurors' minds and find a way to suggest that there was an innocent explanation for how the poison got into his system. New South Wales government medical officer Dr John Laing, who had carried out all the tests on Overton's body, would be a key witness.

Margaret Overton's brother, James Lawrence McClure, was one of the first witnesses and he gave evidence about his brother-in-law's impeccable dress style and told the jury how he had looked in the wardrobe in Overton's bedroom after his death to find his good slacks and riding boots, as well as the money Overton always kept on him, were missing. He also recounted how Dulcie had asked him if Harry could have Overton's three good sports coats and that he answered: 'Oh, I don't think so, Mrs Bodsworth.'

Atwill didn't mention the clothes when he cross-examined McClure. He concentrated on the dangers of Calarsenite, which was fifty per cent arsenic. It became obvious that the defence would try to show that Sam Overton could have ingested it accidentally during the crutching of the sheep, which took place the week before he became ill. The experienced grazier was having none of it. He said he knew that when used on sheep, the Calarsenite was diluted in water and could not be too concentrated or it would be dangerous to the sheep.

Atwill: 'And of course if you did absorb any of the fumes or if you ingested it through the mouth or anything like that, it would be extraordinarily dangerous?'

McClure: 'I don't think so, no.'

Atwill: 'You do not think so?'

McClure: 'I don't think it would be that dangerous, no.'

Atwill: 'That Calarsenite, do you mix it with water?'

McClure: 'Yes, it has to be diluted.'

Atwill: 'And in its raw state it would be more dangerous?'

McClure: 'It would indeed, yes.'

Atwill: 'And if a human being should absorb some of the fumes of that, or even if some of the liquid were put into the mouth or anything like that, it would be extraordinarily dangerous?'

McClure: 'Well, I suppose if some got into the mouth, yes, but I don't think any sensible person would ever ...'

Atwill: 'I quite agree with that. Thank you, Mr McClure.'

Atwill had cut him short. The jury would be told that it is the answers that are evidence, not the questions. Nonetheless, defence lawyers seek to sow the seeds of doubt through the questions they ask.

Then it was Jim's turn to be chipped away at by Atwill.

Atwill: 'Do you know that during this period of crutching, Mr Overton used to assist?'

Jim: 'That is right.'

Atwill: 'And do you recall that during this time when they were doing the crutching they [Overton and Harry Bodsworth] used to leave home early in the morning and come home late at night?'

Jim: 'That is right, yes.'

Atwill: 'And they used to have all their meals down at the woolshed?'

Jim: 'Yes.'

It was Hazel's turn to testify, and her time in the witness box was mercifully brief as she felt her mother's eyes on her. She recounted the conversation when Dulcie told her that Overton wouldn't be at Netallie Station for long and there would be a vacancy. Atwill had only seventeen questions for her, and none of them touched on that conversation or arsenic.

When Allan was called up, Atwill hammered away at him, again concentrating on the long days he had put in on the crutching at the woolshed working side by side with Overton.

Atwill: 'Some you crutch and some you jet?'

Allan: 'Yes.'

Atwill: 'Would you explain to His Honour and the gentlemen of the jury what is involved in jetting?'

Allan: 'Well, jetting involves — it is an arsenic of sheep, to prevent blowfly strike in sheep and it is done around the tail of the sheep and up the back, which you can gulp the fumes very easily.'

Atwill: 'And in fact what you used for this on Netallie Station was a thing called Calarsenite?'

Allan: 'That is right.'

Atwill: 'Which is an arsenic compound?'

Allan: 'That is correct, yes.'

Atwill also pressed Allan on the comment his mother apparently made to him when he went shooting with Overton and Dr Potts. Dulcie had said: 'Allan, while youse are out shooting could you accidentally shoot Sam on the other side of the swamp?' And that when they all came back safe that afternoon, she had said: 'Well, at least you could have done it, Allan.' As Allan spoke, Dulcie could be heard sobbing loudly in the dock.

Atwill: 'You are not sure whether your mother was joking with you or not, are you?'

Allan: 'No, that is something I couldn't say. She may have been joking, but that is what she said to me.'

More than ever before, the three siblings just wanted to get out of there and get home to their families and take in what had happened to Margaret. Jim had his first child to see. They were all on the first plane back to Broken Hill.

The defence argument that Overton could have accidentally inhaled or ingested the arsenic while working with Calarsenite took a battering from Dr Laing despite a spirited cross-examination by Atwill.

Atwill: 'Just going back for one moment to clarify it. Of course you are unable to say first of all whether it [the arsenic] was taken, ingested in powder form or in solution form?'

Laing: 'That is so.'

Atwill: 'Or by fumes from the air?'

Laing: 'I think an amount of this order, I would think it would be impossible to do this by fumes.'

Atwill: 'Are you able to say that definitely?'

Laing: 'I think so, yes.'

Atwill: 'You of course are aware that there are many workers' compensation cases where people working with arsenical compounds receive injuries through fumes?'

Laing: 'Yes, that is so.'

Atwill: 'In large doses?'

Laing: 'Not to this order.'

After his success in getting Dulcie's record of interview with the police excluded from the trial for the Tregenza murder, Atwill tried to have her confession regarding poisoning Overton thrown out on similar grounds — that it had been coerced and she had not spoken freely. After some hours of legal argument in the absence of the jury, the new trial judge, Justice Richardson, came to the opposite decision to that which had been made by Justice Taylor. He said that all Harry had been doing was telling his wife to tell the truth — and allowed the record of interview to be tendered as part of the evidence against Dulcie.

As every one of those catastrophic words, about how she had poisoned Sam with arsenic and couldn't even give a reason for it, were read to the jury by Detective Sergeant John Palmer, Dulcie looked down at the handkerchief she was twisting in her hands.

It was a tall order for Dulcie to convince the jury she was innocent after they had heard her interview with police but once again she made a statement in her defence from the dock. This time her account was rambling, showing nervousness and perhaps even desperation. Dulcie was panicking. She was backed into a corner and the detectives thought they could hear it in her voice.

She said there was no truth in the prosecution's claim that she had wanted to get rid of Overton so that her husband could take charge and manage Netallie Station.

'I never did it. He was a good boss and I would have had no reason to harm him,' she said, the twisted handkerchief now looking like a wet rag.

'He had been working with the shearers and he came back complaining of pains in the stomach. He at no times had a meal with us because he had his own little dining room and we had ours.'

As she had claimed in the Tregenza trial, she said she had been distressed when detectives spoke to her and she would have told them anything: 'I didn't care. They got me so distressed I didn't care what I told them. And I told Mr Kelly he could answer his own questions if he wanted to and I would have signed anything. I would not have cared what it was like. I didn't know what I was letting myself in for.

'As for the accommodation in Melbourne, I was put in a cell on the left-hand side as you go in. All I had was three blankets and I laid on the cement and I never seen a bed there. I was put in a cell on the left-hand side just before you go to where there is a sort of yard affair with rails there, and I stopped there and Mr Ritchie didn't look after us for meals because I felt too upset to eat but he was very good with the meals and so far as the accommodation and the filth in Melbourne it was a disgrace. That's all.'

The jury retired to consider its verdict on Wednesday, 23 August, and the detectives thought the deliberations would not take them long. It had taken the Baron jury less than two hours and the Tregenza jury not much longer. But the day stretched on as Overton's family members along with the police waited for the jury's decision. The defence and prosecution lawyers have their own rooms in which to wait and the detectives could have returned to the main police station — in those days, on the corner just outside the court — but they chose to wait with the family.

There were a few cafés around the courthouse but no one could stray far from the court precincts because the jury could return at a moment's notice. The minutes seemed like hours and, the longer the wait went on, the worry grew that the jury wouldn't get it right.

After four and a half hours, the twelve jurors filed back into the court. They hadn't believed Dulcie. The verdict was guilty. It felt like the courtroom had been holding its breath.

Justice Richardson thanked the jurors and discharged them. He asked Dulcie if she had anything to say before he passed sentence.

'Yes, I do,' she said.

'There was lies told right through the court. I never touched that poor man.'

The judge sentenced her to life and Kelly sent his familiar telegram to Hazel in Broken Hill: 'Saw mother today. It seems like a lifetime.'

It looked like Dulcie's luck had run out. She was finally locked up for life. 'Life', however, didn't mean life, as in 'a lifetime', in New South Wales then and Hazel knew Dulcie would get out one day.

It had taken almost three years and the court saga was almost over. But then the Baron family was rocked by another death.

*

Saturday, 15 June 1968, was going to be a big night at the Buffs Lodge in Broken Hill. The boys — Bill, Allan and Jim — were all members of the Royal Antediluvian Order of Buffaloes, joking that it was the poor man's Masons. Like the Masons, they had their secret codes and mysterious ceremonies but the Masons were for the social elite, not working blokes like them. Allan had got Jim involved when they worked on Kangaroo Island where Allan had reached the third tier of the Buffs as a 'Knight of the Order of Merit'.

The order had nothing at all to do with buffaloes, being named after the popular song of the time that became their anthem when they were formed in 1822, called 'We'll Chase the Buffalo'. Bill, Allan and Jim liked being in the Buffs for the comradeship it offered; they felt they were among friends. As well as raising money for charities, the Buffs looked after each other's families in times of need. The boys also secretly liked the rituals observed by the club, such as the codes which had to be uttered through the narrow slot in the door to get into Broken Hill's Buffs lodge in the centre of town on Argent Street. Women couldn't join, although they had their own female arm. Along with Hazel and Jim's wife Alma, all the wives put up food like sandwiches and sausage rolls for the men.

That Saturday night there was a good spread on and the beers were flowing. It was Jim's turn to be elevated to the 'knighthood'. As a Knight himself, Allan was going to perform the ceremony, driving across from Olary Station that day.

Before he left the station with Joan and the kids, Allan wanted to get a kangaroo to feed the sheep dogs, the kelpies, who would be by themselves for the couple of days the family would be away in Broken Hill. He had a new vehicle he was still getting used to, a second-hand International Scout, which looked like a Jeep. His five-year-old son and one of their dogs jumped in the passenger side to keep him company. Neither Allan nor Jim ever had any problems with slaughtering sheep and 'roos by hand; they had been doing it since they were wet behind the ears.

They hadn't gone more than a kilometre when Allan took a shot at the first 'roo they had seen but he had only winged the animal, which got up and took off. With the rifle reloaded, Allan drove after it but he still hadn't got the hang of the strange gear sticks in the International Scout. As well as the ordinary gear shift, there were another three gear levers including one for high and low range. He had the rifle lodged among the levers and as the vehicle bounced over the ground, it went off and shot him in the liver. He managed to stop the vehicle and collapsed outside. His young son ran back to the homestead for his mother. She was eight months pregnant and couldn't drive. By the time help reached him, Allan had bled to death. He was twenty-six.

The Buffalo ceremony went ahead without Allan; Bill and Jim had figured he was just running late. Until, that is, the knock on the door in Bagot Street later that night. Hazel opened the door to face the police, who delivered the devastating news. They didn't have the phone on so Bill went over to Jim's and let him know.

One of the first things Hazel wondered was if Allan had killed himself. He had been drinking far too much and their mother had him tied up in emotional knots. It had broken his heart. But the police said that it was definitely an accident. They told Hazel that Allan's son was with him and she knew Allan would never have put his son through that. The police also said that no one killed themselves by shooting themselves in the liver.

Then Hazel recalled her mother's weird comments when she had not been told about Margaret's death and funeral: Dulcie had said that if 'anyone else died', she would sue Hazel if she wasn't told about it. It was the strangest thing to say. You would never expect another of your children to die so young. She fleetingly wondered if Dulcie had had some sort of premonition, then she shook that thought out of her mind. She refused to confer that kind of power on her mother.

Allan was buried in the Catholic section at Broken Hill cemetery. Years later when he was a teenager, his oldest son who had been in the car with him could be found just sitting staring at his father's grave.

Once again, Hazel left it up to the police to tell Dulcie about Allan's death. None of the family wanted her at the funeral.

The next time Hazel made the journey to see Dulcie, she realised that she had been right not to have been taken in by her. All Dulcie said about Allan's death was: 'He won't be able to change his story now.' Even at the news of her son's death, she thought first of herself.

CHAPTER ELEVEN

RUBY

DULCIE WORE A SHAPELESS DARK GREEN DRESS BUT THE SEVERE prison clothes were softened by the wide smile on her face as she approached Hazel.

'This is my daughter and she's a nurse and she's come from Broken Hill,' Dulcie boasted to the warder, as inflated as though she were showing off the Queen.

'Shut up, Bodsworth,' the prison guard snapped.

In the grubby bleak visitors' room at Long Bay jail, Hazel flinched. Dulcie was fawning and the guard was just plain rude. It was as though Dulcie were showing off to the school principal and the principal was putting her back in her place. Perhaps in jail, reactions were never on an even keel and emotions were emphasised.

It was about a year since the end of the Overton trial and sitting on green chairs around a table bolted to the floor, mother and daughter spoke about Hazel and Bill's kids — their seven-year-old daughter, three-year-old adopted son and a baby boy just a few months old. Dulcie's grandchildren, whom she had never seen let alone met. They chatted about Bill's family and Jim and Alma. The weather. The journey from Broken Hill. Neither of them mentioned the 'm' word — murder. The closest they got was when Dulcie said life was hard inside and she shouldn't be there.

Hazel reminded her that it was crook on the outside as well.

Hazel had two reasons for going to visit Dulcie. She told herself that, rather than loyalty to Dulcie, it was to keep an eye on her and know what she was up to, but it was also because she was a softie at heart. Even after everything her mother had done, she couldn't leave her to rot.

Dulcie had started to write to her after she lost an appeal against her conviction for murdering Sam Overton. The Court of Criminal Appeal handed down its decision in February 1968, rejecting her lawyers' argument that her record of interview with police had not been made freely and should never have been read to the jury.

'In our opinion there does not appear to be evidence surrounding the making of the statement of the conditions under which it was obtained which justifies a decision that the learned trial judge was bound to hold that unfairness existed or undue pressure was applied or that the appellant was incapable of appreciating the full extent and purpose of her words or of doing justice to herself in her answers.' It was a unanimous decision. Dulcie's lawyers said the High Court would never hear an appeal against a unanimous ruling. It was the end of the road for her. She had to suck it up. She had one life sentence to serve as well as five years for the manslaughter of Ted Baron, both sentences to be served concurrently.

Harry was also in Long Bay but in the men's section, serving his five years.

'I wish I had some margarine to put on my toast,' said Dulcie's first correspondence with her daughter.

'You don't know what it's like in here. The other people get visitors and my family don't care about me. No one ever comes to see me.'

It was real heart-wrenching stuff, totally over the top, but despite that, Hazel felt it pull at her heart strings, even as she realised at the same time that the whole thing was bizarre. As Bill drove her all the way from Broken Hill to Sydney to visit Dulcie, Hazel was wondering how she was going to stop her mother from asking awkward questions such as why did she go to the police? Why did she give evidence? She thought Dulcie would try to coerce her to get her out. She was the one who should have been asking the questions. Why did you kill my father? You bastard, you never cared for us! Where were your hugs? Why go after Sam and Tommy? Why did you put us through all this? But Hazel never asked those questions. Ever. After being the iron lady in the witness box, Hazel couldn't shake the elusive ties between mother and daughter and she had to mentally fight herself to stay in charge.

She was shaking as she walked through the massive wooden doors at Long Bay while Bill waited in their car in the car park, but she never thought about turning back. This is what she had to do just the same as she had had to give evidence against Dulcie. Bill wanted nothing to do with his wicked mother-in-law but never tried to talk Hazel out of visiting her. He supported her as he always had done.

It was the noise that hit Hazel, the shouts bouncing off the concrete walls, the security checks when you went in, showing your identification through the hole in the glass and then securing your handbag in a locker. Just a number, not unlike the people you were going to visit, called out when they were ready to take you through the corridors made of heavy metal bars with barbed wire strung along the top. The banging of the gates, unlocked and locked before the next one was unlocked. The stink of cigarette smoke that permeated the walls and the scrape of chairs as the prisoners got up to greet their visitors.

The visiting room was packed and Hazel took a deep breath as she scanned for her mother. She expected Dulcie to look as old and downcast and even angry as she had the last time she saw her, which was in the courtroom all those months ago. This time, would Dulcie be visibly crushed by the dullness of her daily routine, and the lack of sunshine in the impenetrable brick bunker that was now her stark home, shared with other inmates who were classed as among the country's worst humans, locked up to keep everyone else outside safe?

But Dulcie was grinning and chipper. Hazel was the one who was feeling tense. She braced herself because she knew she had to stop Dulcie taking control once again. She didn't feel ashamed at having once wished her mother had gone to the gallows but her bitterness had subsided. Hazel had spent all those years terrified of what her mother would do, what revenge she would take on Hazel for going to the police, what she would say. Instead, here she was boasting about Hazel probably for the first time in her life.

Hazel had stood up to her and Dulcie knew that. She could see her daughter was not one to mess with. Allan, on the other hand, had never been as strong and Dulcie reserved her venom for him. When he was still alive, Dulcie would send him cruel letters from jail, hammering him and making him feel like the guilty one.

Hazel realised that her mother needed her for the first time in her life. She was under no illusions as to the reason for that — she was the only one in the family who visited Dulcie and Dulcie saw Hazel as her lifeline to the outside world. The woman was as tough and cunning as ever and that was the only reason why she was so nice to Hazel. Hazel didn't really enjoy the visits but she went twice to Long Bay in between February and June 1968 out of a sense of filial duty.

Dulcie hadn't previously had much time or the inclination to read, but behind bars she now had all the time in the world. She learnt to read properly in jail and frequented the library, reading all the newspapers that she could.

She developed a fascination for bushrangers, seeing them as romantic figures thumbing their noses at authority, which she somehow saw herself as doing. Robbing from the rich to give to the poor. In lots of ways, Dulcie was still naïve.

Her favourite bushranger was Ben Hall because she had seen a painting of him when he was young and thought him handsome with his curly brown hair. She was caught up in the romance that he was part of the daring gang who staged the biggest gold robbery in Australian history, the famous Eugowra Gold Escort Robbery. He was still a young man when he died with a 1000-pound bounty on his head after being declared an outlaw, wanted dead or alive.

He was shot dead by police at dawn on 5 May 1865, near Goobang Creek in central western New South Wales at the age of twenty-seven with the circumstances of his death still controversial. Hall was buried in the cemetery at Forbes beneath a simple white headstone.

*

When Silverwater Women's Correctional Centre opened in 1970, Dulcie was one of the first inmates to move into one of its purpose-built twelve living units inside the sprawling complex. She wasn't one for art classes like pottery but she was trusted to have knitting needles and a crochet hook and made baby clothes for the women who had young children in there with them. She had never had a structured life before but she told Hazel that it wasn't as bad as she had feared. Even in jail she got on well for herself and didn't really have a tough time. Just like she had outside, she revelled in having some sort of status. Being in for murder did that for you.

Silverwater was about twenty kilometres outside the CBD and easy to reach for visitors driving from Sydney. However, it was not as convenient for Hazel when Bill was working, and she caught the train or the bus from Broken Hill for her visit once or twice a year.

One day, Dulcie was told there was a Ruby Cavanagh to see her. Ruby knew her mother wouldn't recognise her new name of Shirley McGloin.

She had found out who her mother was through the police when they delved into Dulcie's past as part of their murder investigations. Until then she had lived her life in a vacuum without a birth certificate or knowing the Christian names of her parents, although she knew she had been a Cavanagh. She had few memories of her life before she was abandoned at the orphanage in Wagga Wagga and didn't even think she would recognise her mother again. She had found out where Dulcie was by ringing around the jails. It took a lot of guts for her to go to Silverwater jail and try to talk to the woman who had abandoned her as a little girl. There were enormous pieces missing from the jigsaw puzzle of her life and she hoped Dulcie would help find them. But Dulcie refused to see her and told the prison officers to send her away.

The next time Hazel visited, Dulcie was full of it.

'I told them I wouldn't see her. I'm not interested in Ruby; I'm only interested in you. You are the only one who is sticking by me,' Dulcie told her with an earnest face.

Hazel could see right through her mother's manipulative act. She only told Hazel about Ruby to make her jealous while at the same time trying to curry favour with her by saying that she was more important to her than Ruby. Hazel was over it. She didn't care if Ruby visited or not.

Ruby persevered. A few months later, she went back and was finally reunited with her mother in the drab surrounds of the prison visiting room. Dulcie knew immediately who Ruby was when she walked through the door to where the visitors were already seated at the tables. The two women froze when they first saw each other because they looked so much alike. They discovered that they not only looked alike but they shared similar traits. Ruby's family kept telling her that she was 'flippant', carefree, threw caution to the wind and let whatever was going to happen just happen. A lot like Dulcie.

Ruby had left her husband Gilbert a couple of years earlier but still lived in Yagoona in Sydney's southwest with their three children, son Michael, an adopted son Ian and a daughter she had called Theresa. Ian had made his own headlines in June 1965 when, aged eleven, he ended up at Sydney Airport. With airport security being very lax in those days, he climbed into the cargo hold of a Qantas Boeing 707 before the door was closed — and the plane took off. He didn't mean to stow away, just to have a look around.

After seven hours in the dark and freezing cold, the plane landed in Manila in the Philippines. He was taken to a local hospital, checked over and given hot food, getting a tour of Manila in the meantime.

Qantas flew him home in the proper cabin with a few souvenirs of his unplanned trip, including a Filipino T-shirt and a giant wooden spoon and fork. His parents were told that it was a miracle he had survived. At 30,000 feet he could have frozen to death or his lungs could have burst from lack of pressure. His mother was so relieved to see him that the only punishment dished out was that he couldn't watch TV or use the gifts Qantas had bought him for a month. Dulcie could appreciate the story. Little Ian shared his grandmother's sense of adventure.

Ruby told her mother that her two brothers, Billy, then forty-one, and Ronnie, thirty-seven, were both also living in Sydney and that they were really close to each other. Neither of them ever visited their mother.

*

You would be hard pressed to find anyone who had met one serial killer never mind someone who had been given birth by one and killed by another, but that was Billy Cavanagh. It could be said that he shared his mother's wild streak and lack of respect for the law. Amazingly, both Billy and at least one of his sons also shared Dulcie's penchant for changing their names when it suited them.

Years later, on Saturday, 21 January 1984, the bodies of Billy, fifty-four, and his de facto wife Carmelita Lee, twenty-one, were found in the bedroom of their home in the Sydney suburb of Hoxton Park. The night before, their killer had broken into the house, stripped and gagged Carmelita and tied her hands and feet with a telephone cord before laying her on the couple's waterbed. Then he waited.

Billy, who used the surname Collins as well as Cavanagh, had driven home from a drinking session at his local, the Stop and Rest Hotel at Mt Pritchard, with two bottles of oysters he had bought at the pub. As he walked through the front door, a .22 rifle was pressed to his head and fired twice with another two shots into his neck and the top of his back. His body was then dragged into the bedroom where the rifle was pointed at Carmelita.

The mother of two young children back in the Philippines was also shot four times at point blank range. One of Billy's sixteen children, eighteen-year-old Glen, made the shocking discovery of their bodies in the ransacked bedroom on the Saturday.

When it hit the news, Dulcie rang Hazel to ask if she had any photographs of Billy that she could give to the newspapers. Hazel could see that Dulcie wanted to play the grieving mother role and she was livid. She knew that if the newspapers got onto who Billy's mother was, it would be an even bigger story than it already was. She told her mother in no uncertain terms that she would never speak to her again and Dulcie would be on her own if she dragged the family back into the limelight. Dulcie was suitable chastened with the threat of having no one at all to look after her if Hazel turned her back.

One of Dulcie's grandsons — another of Billy's sons — William, who had changed his surname to Cavanough, arrived at his dad's funeral a week later at Leppington Cemetery in handcuffs and under heavy police guard. The convicted armed robber was midway through serving fourteen years' hard labour at Sydney's Parklea jail after making national headlines two years earlier when he cut a hole in the roof of a moving police van in a spectacular escape while on remand for rape and abduction. He was on the run for less than two months before being caught in Sydney after a bank hold-up and a high-speed chase in which he tried to shoot his way to freedom.

Billy senior had been an amateur boxer, handy with his fists, who ran a successful interstate trucking business. Seven of his semi-trailers were parked out back in the yard of his home. As detectives delved into his background looking for a motive for his murder, they discovered that his trucks had carried millions of dollars' worth of marijuana crops from all over the country for

Robert 'The Godfather' Trimbole. The powerful crime boss was known as the Mr Fix-It for the Mafia in Australia. He had started off as a legitimate businessman born into a Mafia-connected family in Griffith but moved into the far more lucrative marijuana trade. Billy was also known to keep thousands of dollars in cash hidden all over the place at home including inside a lampshade. His murder could have been either a robbery gone wrong or a Mafia hit.

In fact it was neither but it would be another thirteen years before the killer was caught.

In April 1997, across in South Australia, an Adelaide resident was watching a Foxtel TV programme about the man dubbed 'Australia's most wanted', serial killer Lindsay Rose. This person recognised him as Lindsay Lehman who was living in a Bowden boarding house and working as a labourer on the Patawalonga dredging project in the city's west. The person called their local police station and less than twelve hours later Rose was arrested.

'Looks like I won't be in today, boys,' he said as he was arrested at work by heavily armed police. New South Wales detectives flew to Adelaide to seek his extradition on five murders.

Apart from the two murders of Billy Cavanagh and Carmelita Lee, Rose was wanted for the murders of prostitutes Kerrie Pang and Fatma Ozonal, at a massage parlour in the Sydney suburb of Gladesville on Valentine's Day 1994. He had turned up at the brothel to kill Kerrie Pang, one of his former lovers, for a $10,000 contract. Ms Ozonal was shot three times. When Ms Pang, a mother of five, arrived, she was stabbed eighteen times, shot in the right eye, and her throat was cut. Just to make sure, Rose then set the building on fire.

He was also wanted for stabbing to death Reynette Jill Holford who caught him breaking into her millionaire lover's West Ryde mansion, overlooking the Parramatta River, one summer night in 1987. Rose stabbed her thirty-two times and then strangled her as her companion, developer Bill Graf, seventy-nine, slept through the attack.

Rose was a former paramedic who had been hailed as a hero for being one of the first on the scene of Australia's worst rail disaster, in 1977, when a crowded commuter train on its way into Sydney from the Blue Mountains derailed on its way into Granville railway station. It smashed into the supports of a road bridge that collapsed onto two train carriages. Of the passengers, eighty-one died and more than 201 were injured. Rose went on to become a volunteer State Emergency Services worker, a member of the Army Reserve and a licensed pilot. When Rose was twenty-nine, Billy Cavanagh became his first murder victim.

Rose confessed to killing Billy for revenge after Billy had badly beat up a mate of Rose's. He told detectives that Lee was just in the way: 'I had to kill her — she was there!' He pleaded guilty to five previously unsolved murders and was jailed for life without the prospect of parole. He went on to become one of the first six inmates of Goulburn jail's High Risk Management Unit when it was opened in 2001.

*

Dulcie never saw Billy or Ronnie after abandoning them as children. Ruby didn't return for another visit while Dulcie was in jail. Dulcie never told Hazel that Ruby had come back and visited her and Hazel never asked.

Hazel met Ruby once after she had visited Dulcie, but the two half-sisters didn't really hit it off. They arranged to meet in a Sydney park where they would know each other by the colour of the coats they were wearing, Hazel green and Ruby blue. But just as Dulcie and Ruby had recognised each other immediately, so did Hazel and Ruby. They looked like sisters. Both women were anxious to see what the other was like and had been a bit trepidatious about the encounter. In the end, their meeting was cordial but brief. There were never any hard feelings between them but Hazel thought Ruby was too like their mother, Dulcie reincarnated.

In 1972, the South Mine in Broken Hill closed and Hazel and Bill and the family were on the move again. They went to Mansfield in Victoria where Bill got a job at the gold mine, known as the A1 Mine because the gold was 'first class'. One of the country's longest operating mines until it closed in 1992, it was about thirty kilometres outside Mansfield and the miners and their families lived out at the town at the mine, named simply the A1 Mine Settlement. The houses were very basic but the families living in them were only charged fifty cents a week in rent. The mining company charged them in order to create a legal lease so that they could evict them if they wanted.

One day Hazel went to get the washing off the line and discovered it was frozen solid — the first time she had seen ice and snow.

The drive from Mansfield to Silverwater took five hours less than the journey from Broken Hill but the once-a-year visits were still a chore for Hazel. She went because she felt it was the right thing to do and it seemed like she had spent her whole life doing the right thing.

Hazel still never asked about the murders — there was nothing Dulcie could tell her that she didn't already know. But after about five years of meaningless chitchat as Dulcie complained about prison food and Hazel asked her if there was anything she needed, Dulcie said she wanted to tell her about her father. Hazel realised she didn't want to hear it. She didn't want the past; she was over it. She just desperately wanted the future.

'I admit that I did in your father but he was a cruel man, always bad-tempered.' Dulcie was still totally unremorseful. Ted Baron had died not because she and Harry killed him but because he had been cruel and bad-tempered. Hazel didn't feel fear or anger or hatred. She felt an overwhelming sadness.

Dulcie went on to say that of course she had never killed Tommy Tregenza and Sam Overton but she said Tommy was better off dead because he had no one and Overton had been a lonely man whose wife didn't care for him. She went on about never getting a penny from Tommy's will; it was as if he had robbed her. Hazel pushed her plastic chair back and said she would see Dulcie next time.

*

Once Harry had served his five years, he was a free man; but because he had a criminal record, he needed special permission to visit Dulcie. He had vowed never to wear dark green again after all that time in prison garb and was wearing his smart navy suit with a white shirt and colourful tie when he saw Dulcie at Silverwater. The last time she had seen him they had been kissing and cuddling in the tunnels below the Supreme Court at Darlinghurst after being sentenced for killing Ted Baron. She still loved her young Harry and saw that jail had been kind to him. He looked fit and handsome but there was a distance between them now. She put it down to having been separated for all those years and having to put up barriers to survive in jail.

She had no idea that he had fallen in love with someone else — a woman, Pamela, who worked in the prison — and he didn't dare tell her. At least one of them had been rehabilitated.

Harry didn't visit her again and Dulcie was furious when he wrote to say he wanted a divorce. It was the last time she heard from him. Harry moved on to settle into the kind of comfortable loving family life he had never had with Dulcie. He got a job as a storeman and then as a driver, married Pamela and they lived in suburban western Sydney and had three children. When Harry died in June 2016, he was eighty-seven and left a proud legacy of grandchildren and great-grandchildren.

*

After thirteen and a half years behind bars, Dulcie was released and couldn't resist changing her name one more time. Unbeknown to Hazel, she added a touch of exotic to her life by registering on the electoral roll as Doulsie Bodsworth.

Toughened by jail, she was ready for an audience again. When the TV series *Prisoner* hit the small screen in 1979 and went on to become a cult classic around the world, the public would get to meet Dulcie's alter ego. One of the best-loved characters, that mischievous lovable old lag, Lizzie Birdsworth, was based on Dulcie. Bodsworth, Birdsworth ... get it?

CHAPTER TWELVE

DOULSIE BODSWORTH

THE SCONES LOOKED DELICIOUS, THICK AND FLUFFY. GAYLE Hewitt thought it was very Christian for the new lady who had just moved into one of the housing commission units on Roosevelt Avenue in Riverwood to offer to bake for the congregation. Gayle's husband John was the senior pastor at the nearby Revival Life Centre and one of his parishioners had told him about the lonely lady with the gold-framed glasses who always wore a nice frock, 'Doulsie' Bodsworth. John Hewitt reached out to Dulcie just as he did to the other disadvantaged people living in the units, many of them elderly or mentally ill or victims of domestic violence or from non-English-speaking backgrounds. Dulcie had lied that she had been a nurse with the Royal Flying Doctor Service and even donated some crisp white bed sheets to the church for the poor people. Where she got them, nobody knew.

Dulcie attended a couple of services at the Revival Life Centre, which was a Pentecostal church, but when the Hewitts invited her to their latest function she politely declined but offered to make some scones, which were picked up from her by a grateful Gayle

Hewitt. Grateful, that is, until she bit into one. She spat out that first morsel. It tasted of kerosene. The Hewitts knew nothing of Dulcie's real background at the time but they did think she was trying to poison them all.

Had Dulcie purposely tried to poison the congregation? Hazel knew her mother was a 'bugger for kerosene'. She loved the smell of it and used it on rags as a polish. Dulcie always had kerosene in the kitchen and it's possible the scones had been exposed to the fumes and picked up the smell and the taste of it. Then Hazel wondered if her mother had slipped just a bit of the kerosene into the scones to make a good story so she could tell people: 'Well, I only saw them yesterday and they weren't sick then.' Of course it would be a story with her at the centre of it.

The Hewitts didn't accept any more food from her and neither did the local police station. There, her reputation and criminal record had preceded her. The officers had received a general direction that any scones or cakes donated by Mrs Bodsworth to them or the local magistrates were not to be eaten.

When the public housing was built in Riverwood in the 1950s, the streets were named after United States presidents, cities and states. Dulcie, a model prisoner, was released in 1977 after serving thirteen years. Her parole officer Nancy found her a nice little unit in Washington Street, named after the first US president. Dulcie hated it and she hated one of her neighbours. She had to walk past this man's front door every day and as she did so he always called out an abusive name for her.

She was still an arsonist at heart. This time it was not for murder, like the killing of Tommy Tregenza, or for revenge, like the time she burnt down the house and shed at Burragan Station. It was simply to get her own way. She stuffed newspapers into the electric bar heater in the kitchen and started a blaze in her own unit.

Hazel and Bill and the family had been on the move again, this time from Victoria to a town in the Central West of New South Wales where Hazel got a job as a nurse at the town's hospital. Bill worked as a machine operator with Telstra. Hazel was at work when she got a call from her mother's parole officer to say that Dulcie's unit had gone up in flames. The unit was trashed but Dulcie was okay. She had only suffered burns to her hands while she tried to put out the fire and save things. Putting it out! Hazel suspected straight away what had happened. Sure enough, Dulcie was happily moved into the second unit at Roosevelt Avenue — named after the twenty-sixth President of the United States — leaving her abusive neighbour behind.

She liked this second unit because it was on the ground floor at the front of the complex so she could see who was coming and going. Nancy the parole officer helped Dulcie get some replacement second-hand furniture from Vinnies and when Hazel visited her for the first time six months after her release from jail, Dulcie had set herself up nicely. The unit stank of kerosene, which Dulcie had been using as polish. Bill gave Hazel a lift from their country town but he still was not ready to see Dulcie so he waited in the car while Hazel spent the afternoon with her mother. She had brought Dulcie some fresh clothes and some kitchen utensils — everyone likes new kitchen utensils.

Harry was gone so Dulcie was on her own with Hazel, the only family who visited her. The way Dulcie treated her daughter, you would think she had always been the apple of her eye instead of the person who put her behind bars.

So Dulcie settled into the retirement unit where her new best friend was Margaret, a widow with no family but some money and valuables. Just the kind of person Dulcie liked. A bit like a female Tommy Tregenza.

Dulcie read in a newspaper about plans for a new TV series based in a women's jail with the slogan: 'If you think prison is hell for a man, imagine what it's like for a woman'. She still showed no remorse for killing three people and wrote to the production company making the series, the Reg Grundy Organisation, offering to tell them her story. Bizarrely, after spending the first half of her life hiding behind false names and in strange towns, she was suffering from publicity deprivation. She had got used to being a bit of a kingpin in Silverwater. She also had heaps of new stories to tell from her time behind bars but no one to tell them to. After all, she couldn't tell Margaret about her real past, not about being a serial killer.

So Dulcie sat down with one of the writers from Grundy and what she told them was a story that was no closer to the truth than she ever told anyone. She told them she had been in jail for something she had never done and rolled out the sob story about betrayal and having to bring up her children herself. The production company did their own homework on her and knew there was more to her past than she let on, but they knew she would make a great character in the series. After thirteen years behind bars, she knew a lot about how to get through the day in prison and prison slang.

Dulcie gave herself the grand-sounding title of 'consultant' to the production. Watching the series today, *Prisoner* looks its age but decades before programmes like *Orange is the New Black*, it was a TV trailblazer focusing on the lives of the female inmates and the officers who kept them in line in the fictional Wentworth Detention Centre.

The characters were mainly clichés, like the butch and violent lesbian, a yuppie out of her element and the firm-but-fair governor. The producers took bits and pieces of Dulcie's past to build the

Lizzie Birdsworth character. Lizzie was behind bars because of a poisoning on a sheep station, except that Lizzie was serving a sentence for poisoning four sheep shearers who she cooked for — not the station manager, as Dulcie had done. It turned out in later episodes that, unlike Dulcie, Lizzie was innocent of the poisoning. Lizzie gave up a daughter at birth and when she got out of jail, she burnt down the house where she was living to stop it from being sold. Veteran actress Sheila Florance became a household name for her performance as the mischievous Lizzie, one of the best-known characters, who appeared in almost every episode of the soap opera, 403 in all.

The real murderer the character was based on was never revealed. It had been years since Dulcie's case had been in the news and there was no internet or Google in those days. The real life killer and the woman who portrayed her met a couple of times but there were few of Dulcie's mannerisms in Sheila Florance's brilliant portrayal of Lizzie.

When Hazel went down to Sydney to clear out her mother's unit years later, she found signed photos of nearly all the *Prisoner* crew such as the Grundys, Peta Toppano, who had played one of the inmates, and a number of stars who had done concerts for the show. There was even an autographed photograph of the pop star Sandy Shaw, who was of the ilk of entertainers like Col Joye and Johnny O'Keefe. Hazel also found receipts from Grundys who had been paying Dulcie good money for her advice. One receipt was for $500, a lot of money in those days. It was obvious that Dulcie had thoroughly enjoyed herself as a 'consultant'.

One of the few people who knew about Dulcie's past was Sister Carmel, the full-time chaplain at the Riverwood retirement unit complex. Hazel found her to be a spirited, friendly person, and even more importantly, she was wide awake to Dulcie's antics.

One day Hazel got a call from Sister Carmel to say that she feared Dulcie was up to her old tricks because Margaret had been sick and was going downhill. Hazel was terrified. She couldn't cope with another murder. She thought about calling Del Fricker but Sister Carmel calmed her down and said she would keep an eye on the two 'friends'.

One day, when the Sister tried to visit Margaret, Dulcie told her that Margaret was asleep and had asked to be left alone. Sister Carmel got a key to Margaret's flat and was horrified to find rope and torn-up sheets tied to chairs like a jigsaw across the room to keep Margaret away from the front door. Margaret was in bed and very weak. Dulcie said the rope and sheets were meant to give Margaret something to hold on to when she got up. Whatever the truth, the chaplain called for an ambulance and at the hospital, pathology tests showed Margaret had overdosed on the sleeping tablet Mogadon.

It turned out that Dulcie and Margaret had the same doctor. Dulcie would take him her infamous cakes and say Margaret wanted her to pick up her prescriptions. Hazel was furious that the doctor had been taken in like this and called him up to tell him about Dulcie's past. He didn't believe her until Sister Carmel backed her up. Margaret recovered and went to a nursing home where she didn't see Dulcie again and died peacefully two years later, aged ninety.

For the next ten years, Dulcie amused herself conning people and picking fights with other residents of the retirement units. Some of them were tough cookies and Dulcie, being manipulative and liking to be top dog, had difficulty convincing them that she should rule the roost. She regularly had little 'accidental' fires in her unit, just because she liked the drama, and Hazel would visit to find burn marks on the carpet or the couch. Dulcie dug out a few of her hard-luck stories including how her husband had drowned and she had raised their four children herself. 'Oh, Dulcie,' people would say. 'You have had such a lot of bad luck.' And Dulcie would revel in their sympathy.

When Hazel visited her mother in late 2003, she had to go to the office to sign some papers, and she was amazed when the staff almost laid out the red carpet for her.

'Well, aren't we in the presence of royalty,' one of them said.

The former real estate agent Mary Donaldson of Tasmania had just become engaged to Crown Prince Frederik of Denmark and Dulcie had told everyone the Bodsworths were related to the Donaldsons. She claimed that her family was related to the 'Donaldsons of Tasmania'.

'Your mum's such a dag. We love her. She told us about her and Mary!' the office staff said.

Inside, Hazel was thinking what a lying old bitch Dulcie was but she couldn't deny that she was entertaining. She decided not to put the office staff straight and just smiled secretively.

The office staff thought Hazel was a hospital matron because that is what Dulcie had told them, boasting about how successful her daughter was.

Then there was Jim Courier. Dulcie told everyone they were distantly related and even convinced herself it was the truth. It was his ginger hair. When Hazel looked at the US tennis ace she did think that was what her brother Allan would have looked like if he were still alive. She still thinks of Allan whenever she sees Courier on the TV, usually during Wimbledon. Although there is no evidence they are related, Dulcie even has Hazel wondering if it is true.

Dulcie still liked to be liked and continued her knack of being liked for someone she wasn't. She loved talkback radio and always had it turned on in the background. Like many older people whose lives have shrunk to the confines of their own homes, her conversations were mainly about what other people had been saying over the airwaves. She became so familiar with the radio hosts that she felt they were her friends and drove them mad with her calls and comments, a lot of which were racist. Her favourite talkback hosts were John Laws and Ray Hadley, who eventually got wise to her and refused to take her calls. She argued many times on air with 2GB's Brian Wilshire on his night-time radio programmes. Eventually, Dulcie took to using several different names when she called the stations but she never managed to trick the producers and get them to put her on air.

Bill had begun to make forays into Dulcie's unit when Hazel visited once or twice a year, unable to maintain his hostility. Always the gentle soul that Hazel married, he was able to wipe the past and start from today no matter how badly people had treated him. Dulcie realised Hazel was still wary of her and decided to make Bill her best friend. She was shameless and Hazel watched on amused as her mother all but flirted openly with the son-in-law she had never approved of. Dulcie soon found out Bill's weak spots — food and jokes — and, despite himself, Bill found he had fun in her company. One thing Hazel never did when visiting her mother was eat any of her home baking; she always said she wasn't hungry and packed her own sandwiches to eat later in the car. One day Dulcie insisted they take one of her apple pies home with them. Hazel handed it to the staff in the office — then worried if it was a 'safe' one. It was and no one became ill.

Dulcie began to love publicity. She dressed dolls to raffle for charity and she featured in the local paper several times as she handed over the dolls to the local fire brigade or ambulance station or another good cause. Of course the articles never mentioned her real past. She made cakes for the local state MP, Morris Iemma, before he went on to become Premier of New South Wales in 2005. One year some of the locals got together and approached him to put Dulcie up for an Order of Australia. At one word from the police, the suggestion was slapped down.

While Dulcie's two oldest sons Billy and Ronnie still showed no interest in ever seeing their mother again, Ruby — or Shirley McGloin — couldn't quite let her mother go. Mother and daughter had not kept in touch after that one time they met at Silverwater jail. In 1984, Ruby's son Michael McGloin registered with the Salvation Army to see if they could track Dulcie down for his mother. One night he was watching TV when the Salvation Army rang to say they thought they had found Dulcie but they couldn't hand out her contact details. Michael told them to pass on his mother's details to Dulcie who rang and said she would like to see Ruby.

This time Ruby took Michael along to meet his grandmother. Unlike the first meeting, this one was not a success. As a young man, Michael didn't really want to sit around in the unit and didn't warm to the grandmother he had never known. Ruby felt uncomfortable and only stayed for about fifteen minutes. They didn't meet again and Ruby died in 2013.

As Dulcie got older and her health worsened, she would call Hazel day and night, trotting out sob stories and saying she wanted to live with her. She was unwell. She was lonely. But Hazel stood firm. She had her family to protect.

In cries for help — or attention — Dulcie stopped taking her heart and blood pressure medications as prescribed. She would be listening to the radio, drop off to sleep, wake up and take her tablets, then fall asleep and take them again when she woke up next. A carer checked on her every day and one day in 2006, Dulcie was rushed to hospital semi-conscious with signs of a stroke. It turned out to be an accidental overdose of the medication and Hazel and Bill drove to Sydney to visit her.

Hazel discovered her mother had been creating havoc. She had not been allowing the carers to cook or clean for her — Dulcie said they were lazy and she didn't trust them. Her unit was filthy and stank of urine and Hazel told the staff that Dulcie could not go back there. The reply was that it was Dulcie's choice whether to move out, so they took her back to see how she would manage. As they waited, the staff asked Dulcie to make them a cup of tea so they could check that she was capable of living alone. Dulcie fiddled about with the stove for some time before telling them it didn't work. She appeared vague and disorientated. So it was back to hospital for her.

Hazel visited her in hospital the next day and Dulcie told her that she had outsmarted them all. 'They took me home but I was too smart for them. They wanted a cuppa and I pretended the stove didn't work when it really did.' Hazel thought yet again how she would never understand Dulcie's mind. One side of her was funny and kind but the other was so cool and calculating in planning her crimes, however big or small. Hazel was sure that even then, if someone had known what Dulcie was planning and had challenged her, she would have been horrified at being found out.

Hazel shopped around to find a nursing home for Dulcie and found a suitable one at Blakehurst, only fifteen minutes from the Riverwood unit. Dulcie was savage when told the news. She refused to go. She wanted to go home with Hazel, full stop. Hazel persuaded her that it was only for a short time until she was stronger. The day after Dulcie moved in, Hazel asked the staff if she and her mother could talk in private. Dulcie became excited, thinking Hazel was going to take her home. Instead, Hazel had become the calculating one. For the first time in sixty years, she felt safe and strong enough to say to her: 'Mum, you can't live with me, I can't trust you. I don't know what you might do to me or my family.'

Dulcie started with the high-handed mother talk: 'You can't speak to me like that!'

Hazel very firmly replied: 'Yes, I can and this is why.' Then she unveiled her secret weapon.

She showed her the newspaper clippings she had brought along that covered the years of Dulcie's crimes. Hazel was fully prepared to show them to staff and reveal the real Dulcie but she much preferred to use them as blackmail. It worked.

Dulcie was horrified and demanded to know where they had come from. For a moment she appeared to crumble; she put her head in her hands and said: 'Well, I'll just have to kill myself.' Hazel was finished with the histrionics and amazed Dulcie by telling her: 'Well, that's your choice.' Then she turned around, left the turmoil behind and went home with Bill.

Dulcie soon had the staff of the nursing home eating out of her hand. All her life she had prided herself on appearing 'respectable' and she never swore. But either there was a new Dulcie or she had just always suppressed the real Dulcie because she suddenly had quite a tongue on her. Many of the nurses were big Maori or Fijian women and Dulcie always commented on their size. She would shout at them things like: 'Get your fat arse over here, the phone's ringing.' Or when the doctor would visit, she yelled: 'Here comes the doctor; get off your arse and go and talk to him.' The doctor would laugh, the nurses would laugh, and Dulcie laughed along with them, pleased to have an audience again.

One day Hazel got a call from a couple of Dulcie's Riverwood friends that took her by surprise. The two women demanded to know how she could do this to a good, decent mother. They said it was obvious that Dulcie had been right when she said her daughter and her family didn't care about her when she had done so much for all her children! Dulcie had told her friends that Hazel had dumped her at the nursing home with no clothes and had taken all her money. Hazel had had enough. She countered by asking one of the women if she knew that Dulcie was a compulsive liar and had served time for murder.

'How low will you go to denigrate such a good person,' Dulcie's friend retorted.

Some weeks later Hazel received letters from both of the friends saying they had found out the truth about Dulcie's past and reprimanding Hazel for not telling them because their 'lives could have been in danger'.

Barely a day went by when there was not a call to Hazel from the nursing home to say Dulcie had done this or that, always for attention. Hazel went on to remind everyone yet again that while Dulcie was witty, she was still dangerous and forever a fire bug. One day a nurse walking past her room saw her up on the bed trying to push waste paper into the electric strip heater on the wall when she was supposed to be confined to a wheelchair. The nurse stopped her before there was a fire. Dulcie told Hazel she had just been bored and thought it would get her thrown out of the nursing home. It was a wake-up call for the head doctor at the home. He called Hazel and she got Bill to drive her to Sydney. She took along some of those same old newspaper clippings about Dulcie, feeling she should tell him the whole story. After reading that he had a serial killer in his care, the doctor put his head down on the desk and said: 'How did I get this lucky?'

He said he had to put the safety of the other residents of the nursing home first and asked for Hazel's permission to restrain her mother. She signed her mother up for every kind of restraint, chemical and physical. She told the doctor: 'Just do whatever you need to.'

Dulcie hated it at first. There was a belt around her waist that tied her into the wheelchair. On the back of the chair was a chain with a clip that was fastened onto a hook in the wall of the office. It was the only way they could keep an eye on her and keep everyone safe. After a while Dulcie quite enjoyed being at the centre of what was happening and watching everyone come and go from the office. She was given extra medication which made her quite mellow and pleasant and even the head doctor, who had worried about having a serial killer as a patient, was won over by her.

Eventually, in 2006 at the age of ninety-seven, Dulcie moved back to live not with her daughter but as close as she had been for decades. The hospital where Hazel had worked, just a few steps from her home, was old and when it closed down, it was converted into an aged care nursing home and she managed to get Dulcie a room there. She was flown from Sydney in an air ambulance. She had started to slow down but her mind was still sharp and her health fairly good, and she liked to sit outside the front of the nursing home in the afternoons and chat to people walking past.

By then both Hazel and Bill had retired so they had plenty of time to visit Dulcie, taking cakes and pies with them on their visits because Dulcie no longer had the facilities to bake for herself.

In the first few days of September 2008, Hazel noticed her mother had slowed right down. With a lifetime's experience of nursing, she knew the signs when people began the process of dying. For Dulcie, it began on a Tuesday. Hazel sat by her mother's bedside until late that night and again on the Wednesday night. By then Dulcie was semi-conscious and needed oxygen to help her breathe.

By the Thursday, Dulcie was really low. At one point she squeezed Hazel's hand and asked: 'Is that you, Hazel?' Hazel stayed at her bedside until 2 am and was back there by 7 am on the Friday when she gave her mother a sponge bath and dressed her in a fresh nightie. Hazel knew this would be the final day.

At 10 am, Hazel wanted a cup of tea and on the spur of the moment before she left Dulcie's room, she leant over her and said: 'Mum, I'm going for a cup of tea. Why don't you close your eyes and go to heaven? Your mother and father have opened the gates. They are waiting for you. You know it is a nice place where everyone forgives everyone. If you have it in your heart, forgive us and we have it in our hearts to forgive you. So just close your eyes.'

Hazel was sure her mother had heard. She looked peaceful for the first time in her life.

Dulcie was breathing hard when Hazel got back to the room fifteen minutes later. Hazel placed her hand over one of her mother's hands and Dulcie flicked her eyes open.

'Hazel, are you there?' she asked and Hazel replied that she was. Then Dulcie took a deep breath and closed her eyes. She was ninety-nine. To Hazel it seemed as if Dulcie had asked her permission to die.

Hazel was broken-hearted. When she had once thought that her mother deserved to go to the gallows, now she was left feeling desolate. She had been cranky, hurt and bitter in the 1960s. Now she thought of all the sad things that both she and her mother had gone through and all the bad — and some good — times that had been part of their lives. She felt empty that it was all over. She thought about her father and Tommy Tregenza and Sam Overton and wondered just for a split second if Dulcie would see them in her next life.

But Hazel also felt relief — relief that she no longer had to worry about what Dulcie was up to and who might get hurt. It hit her that few people had lived such tortured lives but she no longer had to bear the burden of responsibility. For almost the first time in her life, Hazel could relax.

She had already brought clothes to the hospital to lay out her mother in. She had bought her a new pink flannelette nightie with lace down the front, pink and white striped socks and a pink shawl. Dulcie, who had never felt the cold when she was younger, liked to have her shoulders and feet covered because she had started to feel the chill. Hazel bathed her mother again before dressing her for the last time.

Hazel and Bill gave Dulcie a simple but respectable Salvation Army funeral. Hazel did not want to be defined by her dysfunctional mother and by her life but by the worthwhile things that had happened in her own life. Yet as she stood at the front of the chapel and gave the eulogy, she knew that the ties between mother and daughter can never really be broken. There were twenty-one grandchildren and dozens more great-grandchildren that Hazel knew of. She thought it would be difficult to think what to say about Dulcie's life — which bits to leave in and which bits to leave out — but the words, which she had written down in advance, had come to her easily.

She had them made up in a printed leaflet with a recent photograph of Dulcie on the front looking, as she had her whole life, as if butter wouldn't melt in her mouth. In her wheelchair, with a halo of white fluffy hair and a bright smile, she looked like the kindest and sweetest old lady.

'She touched many lives. Some would say she was witty and generous and a good friend and you would be correct. Some would say she was difficult and out of touch. You would also be correct,' Hazel read out.

'She was a tough cookie at times and us kids knew about the school of hard knocks. We know that our past is not our future and what we see depends on mainly what we look for, but life is not about how fast you run or how high you jump but how well you bounce.

'In the name of cricket she had many runs on the board and probably more than enough innings but last week she thought I am so weary and it's the end of my day so I will leave you and go into the next room.

'It is peaceful and full of joy and one day I will greet all of you so don't weep because I have gone but smile because I have been.

'Now the radio has stopped, the crochet hook is still, the oven is turned off and the scones are no more. Rest in peace, Mother, and God bless you.'

There had not been many people to invite to the service. Hazel didn't bother letting her mother's two mixed-up 'friends' know because they would have thought their lives to be in danger if they had turned up. She had lost touch with Harry, and Dulcie never mentioned him after learning he had remarried. Allan and Margaret were dead. The small congregation was made up of immediate family including Hazel's brother Jim, his wife Alma and Hazel's friends. Hazel reminded them that her mother's friend Morris Iemma had left parliament on the same day Dulcie died — 5 September 2008. As Dulcie had been a great cook, Hazel figured her mother would have approved of the spread that was put on for the wake in her honour.

When it came to cremating Dulcie, Hazel couldn't find a birth certificate because there had never been one. All she had was the Centrelink document in which Dulcie had revealed her true age. A stickler for protocol, the undertaker said he had to have the paperwork before he could organise anything. Hazel told him point blank that he would have to keep Dulcie in the fridge because he would never get a birth certificate.

So Dulcie was cremated, but she had left Hazel with one final burden. What to do with the ashes? Dulcie had said she wanted to be buried close to Ben Hall the bushranger in Forbes General Cemetery, because they were both innocent and had both been badly treated. It was lost on her that while Hall was infamous, he had never killed anyone, while Dulcie was a serial killer. They were both outlaws in their own way.

Forbes General Cemetery on Bogan Gate Road is not only home to the bushranger's grave but a resting place for a who's who of Australian bush history. There is the grave of Rebecca Shield, a great-grand-niece of Captain Cook, who died in 1902 aged eighty-four, and Kate Foster, who was Ned Kelly's sister. All this history makes Ben Hall's final resting place one of the country's most-visited cemeteries. It would have been totally illegal to bury Dulcie's ashes there.

Instead, her ashes were scattered to the wind in the Forbes vicinity. Hazel thought that if her mother and Ben Hall met up, they might just get along and have a good laugh. Not long after Dulcie's death, a white fence with a gate was put up around Ben Hall's grave. Later a padlock went on the gate. Hazel never figured out whether it was to keep Ben Hall in — or Dulcie out.

EPILOGUE

THEIR SPRAWLING SINGLE-STOREY HOME WAS ALWAYS FULL OF children and noise and the smell of baked dinners as Hazel and Bill added foster kids to their swelling brood. The kitchen, with its wood-burning fire and a big dining table with a cluster of chairs, opened onto the living room, where there was always a dog or two sharing the comfy couches or panting in the sun. The back garden was like one big playground.

Like the first house the young couple had bought in Wilcannia, this one in country NSW had a big porch and Hazel liked to sit out there with a cup of tea in the summer evenings. Conveniently, the house was just around the corner from the hospital where Hazel worked until the day she retired.

Despite Hazel having had some misgivings when she married Bill 60 years ago, worrying about what love felt like and wondering if this was it, the couple stuck together like glue their whole lives. Hazel certainly wasn't going to let Dulcie ruin the second half of her life as she had done the first half.

Photographs of the couple's four children — three boys and

a girl — and their six grandchildren at various ages, covered the walls. Hazel never hid from her children the truth about their grandmother, although it wasn't something they spoke about often.

One day when Hazel was asked by them how she could have had anything to do with her mother after Dulcie had murdered Hazel's father, Hazel had an answer that summed up, as only she could, her relationship with Dulcie: I don't hate her; I don't even dislike her. She was like a neighbour and I did the right thing by her,' Hazel would say. After all those years of anguish and guilt, mixed with loyalty and disgust, she made it sound so simple.

The home she and Bill created was warm and welcoming. For many of the 101 foster children in total that the amazing couple opened up their hearts and lives to over the years, it was the only time these youngsters had been able to relax and feel safe. Even if they were in her care for only a few weeks or months, Hazel was determined to give each of them everything she never had: comfort, love, a chance to learn, and an opportunity to enjoy being kids. She cared about what they said, what they did and what they thought. A lot of those children, now grown up with their own families, still call Hazel and Bill 'Mum and Dad'.

The tough upbringing that had shaped Hazel's character and made her brave and strong enough to take on her mother also made her want to do something for others. Fostering children made her feel as though she was making some amends for the damage her mother had wreaked on other people's lives.

'I always thought that,' Hazel said. 'I thought if I'm doing this, I'll make up for just a little bit of what she had done.'

And she did this even though it was not *her* obligation to do anything. But that's Hazel: resilient, funny, cheeky, passionate and inspiring but, above all, decent and always responsible. A good mother — and a good daughter.

Acknowledgements

This book would never have happened without Jeff Herdigan, who started the ball rolling by telling Hazel that it 'should be a book'. He has been a tremendous supporter and adviser.

The first outline for what became this book was typed from Hazel's longhand by her friend Pat Hodson. Pat handled this job with dexterity and should be proud to have been able to decipher Hazel's handwriting.

A lot of the legwork was done by Hazel's friends Michelle Quigley and Val Smith. Thanks also go to journalist John Rolfe, whose late mother had worked with Hazel and who got in touch with Janet Fife-Yeomans after being contacted by Ray and Monica Sanderson. His approach led to a front-page article by Janet in the *Daily Telegraph* and began the friendship between Janet and Hazel.

Hazel Baron's memories form the basis of this book but the full story of Dulcie Bodsworth's life was pieced together from a variety of sources, which included court documents and personal interviews. No-one spoken to had forgotten her even after all these years.

The authors would like to thank all the unflaggingly patient media advisers with the State's courts who persisted in digging out relevant court judgments and transcripts that still exist. They are Georgie Loudon, Angus Huntsdale, Lisa Miller and Sonya Zadel.

Michael McGloin was happy to share his memories of his mother, Ruby, to set the record straight.

Thanks also go to retired Broken Hill police officers Gus Williams and Bob Wighton. Although they never met Dulcie or Hazel, they certainly remembered them and Ray Kelly.

Tommy Tregenza has no family left but Sam Overton certainly does, and the authors would like to thank Jeremy McClure, who now runs Netallie Station, keeping it in the family for future generations. His recollections of 'Bodsworthville' are gratefully included.

Journalist turned farmer Bessie Blore, who farms Burragan Station and whose husband's family have run merinos on the same land for generations, generously shared the history she had learned about Dulcies and Harry's time on the property.

The authors also drew on knowledge from books including *Early Days of Korumburra* by Dr K Bowden, *The Prince and the Premier* by David Hickie, and *Whoever Fights Monsters* by Robert K Ressler.

Janet Fife-Yeomans is a bestselling author and award-winning journalist who has worked in newspapers and television in Australia and her native England. She is a leading investigative writer on crime and legal issues, and is currently chief reporter for Sydney's *Daily Telegraph*. This is her ninth book.